Dreams & Emotional Adaptation

A Clinical Notebook for Psychotherapists

Dreams & Emotional Adaptation

A Clinical Notebook for Psychotherapists

ROBERT LANGS, M.D.

ZEIG, TUCKER & CO., INC., PUBLISHERS
PHOENIX, ARIZONA

Library of Congress Cataloging-in-Publication Data

Langs, Robert, 1928–
    Dreams and emotional adaptation : a clinical notebook for psychotherapists / Robert Langs.
        p.   cm.
    Includes bibliographical references and index.
    ISBN 1-891944-05-3
    1. Dreams—Therapeutic use.   2. Adjustment (Psychology)
3. Communicative psychotherapy.   I. Title.
    RC489.D74L36   1999
    616.89'14—dc21   98-38986
                                                                      CIP

Copyright © 1999 by Zeig, Tucker & Co., Inc.

All rights reserved. No part of this book may be
reproduced by any process whatsoever without
the written permission of the copyright owner.

Published by

ZEIG, TUCKER & CO., INC.
1928 East Highland, Suite F104-607
Phoenix, Arizona 85020

Manufactured in the United States of America

10   9   8   7   6   5   4   3   2   1

CONTENTS

Introduction   vii

Part One: Dreams as Psychobiological Communications

Chapter One: An Adaptive Definition of Dreams   3

Chapter Two: Dreams and Nondynamic Theories of the Mind   18

Chapter Three: Dreams and Psychodynamic Models of the Mind 30

Chapter Four: Dreams and an Adaptive Model of the Mind   47

Chapter Five: The Structure and Adaptive Functions of Dreams 63

Chapter Six: An Evolutionary History of Dreams   82

Part Two: Dreamwork

Chapter Seven: The Triggers for Dreams   115

Chapter Eight: The Manifest Contents of Dreams   135

Chapter Nine: The Encoded Contents of Dreams   157

Chapter Ten: Dream Psychotherapy   179

References   195

Index   201

Introduction

It can be said that dreams offer a remarkable window into both the surfaces and the depths of the emotional mind and of human emotional life, its issues and its adaptations. For this reason, therapeutic work with dreams—so-called dreamwork—has been a feature of psychotherapy practice from its origins in the landmark work of Freud (1900) to the present day. Over the years, our understanding of dreams has become increasingly sophisticated and effective, as have the techniques developed to interpret their meanings. Nevertheless, prevailing approaches to dreamwork are not without their problems and limitations. The present book offers solutions to these difficulties.

Dreams owe their importance in understanding the vicissitudes of emotional life and the process of psychotherapy not so much to their being dreamed in the altered state of consciousness of sleep, as to the fact that their imagery and verbal report almost always are in *storied or narrative* form. The development of language in humans, and with it, the ability to weave tales, has provided us with a unique mode of communication that serves emotional adaptation in invaluable ways. Intensely layered with meaning, capable of both revealing and concealing, possessing both truth value and deception, the dreams of patients can be explored, unraveled,

vii

Introduction

and used therapeutically by psychotherapists of every persuasion.

My strategy for this book is to offer a new method of working with dreams that maximizes the value of dreamwork and the insights it renders. My intention is to do so in light of our current understanding of the design and operations of the emotional mind—*the emotion-processing mind,* as I call it (Langs, 1995a). In this context, I offer an *adaptation-centered* approach to dreams that considers in depth the means by which they reflect both conscious and unconscious modes of coping.

The goal is to discover ways to access, understand, and interpret the most powerful meanings of dream experiences in ways that are of practical, clinical value to psychotherapists regardless of their basic orientation. Even therapists who seldom work with dreams, or who do so in limited ways, will find it extremely helpful to learn how to access the emotionally compelling deeper meanings and implications of dream material. Such knowledge is of value for a general perspective on the nature of emotional life and the therapy process, and it also can be exceedingly useful at times of clinical crisis.

Main Features of the Book

While this book is intended for therapists of all backgrounds, the concepts and dreamwork described stem from a particular clinically derived, new paradigm of psychoanalysis and dynamic psychotherapy called *the communicative approach* (Langs, 1982, 1992a, 1993; Smith, 1991, 1998). This approach to emotional life and psychotherapy is fundamentally and strongly adaptive in nature, and it presumes both conscious and unconscious efforts at coping in response to

Introduction

emotionally charged environmental events, including communications from, and actions by, significant others.

The communicative approach has developed a deep understanding of the adaptive operations of the emotion-processing mind, the *mental module* that has evolved for dealing with emotionally charged experiences (Langs, 1995a, 1996b). The book, therefore, is fashioned in light of an appreciation of the fundamental, universal architecture and operations of this mental module, which is, of course, shaped and modified by personal experience. This grounding will provide depth to the dreamwork techniques described.

The book is designed as a practical guide to how to work effectively with the surface, as well as the most meaningful depths, of dreams, as they clarify and give meaning to both successful and unsuccessful emotional adaptations. We will study basic modes of listening to and formulating patients' material, and of intervening. And we also will avail ourselves of recent investigations into the evolutionary history of dreaming and dreams, as they shed light on present-day emotional adaptations and the functions of dream communications (Langs, 1996b).

In grounding the book in a strong adaptive approach, we will examine in detail both the specific nature of emotionally charged impingements or *environmental events* (a term I use to refer to incidents and/or communications stemming from both material and physical happenings and the behaviors of living entities), and how we as humans, and as patients in particular, respond to these impingements. This microscopic study of the conscious and unconscious meanings of environmental inputs and adaptive responses will reveal aspects of emotional adaptation that cannot be seen when viewed in the context of the more general and inherently vague approaches to this area. Nature turns out to be very different when de-

Introduction

fined broadly as compared with when it is carefully examined in detail.

The Levels of Meaning in Dreams

There are, of course, many layers of meaning in every dream. This property of dreams has led to a variety of approaches to understanding the implications of dream material and interpreting a dream's manifest and latent contents. By and large, each of these formulations, be it psychodynamic, cognitive, existential, or otherwise, has a measure of validity and utility. Each is supported by—and, in turn, supports—a theory of and an approach to psychotherapy. Nevertheless, it should be recognized that there is, as yet, no generally accepted means of deciding which formulations are in error, which are trivial, and which are of major significance emotionally and curatively.

In this book, we explore that issue and arrive at a means of encoded or deep unconscious validation that can serve as a guide to dreamwork. We will look at the surface of dreams, their so-called manifest contents, and explore their implications. But we also will examine the *latent contents* of dreams, with special emphasis on one form of such contents, namely, *encoded meanings*. These meanings are camouflaged in the dream's surface images and themes (and the images and themes stemming from narrative associations to dreams). Dreams are, then, a unity of both unencoded and encoded messages, and each level of meaning deals with distinctive adaptive issues, and does so in terms of distinctive adaptive responses.

Clinical evidence indicates that the encoded meanings dis-

Introduction

guised in dreams are reflections of adaptive responses that involve subliminal or unconscious perception and unconscious adaptive processing in response to anxiety-provoking, emotionally charged incidents, so-called triggering events. The experiences and meanings conveyed in this manner are most certainly among the most powerful causes of emotional maladaptations, and also play a role in the success of coping efforts and emotional growth. Thus, an understanding of the role of dreams in patients' conscious and unconscious adaptive efforts will be a decisive contribution of this book.

Additional Perspectives

As a form of narrative, dreams are at the pinnacle of human communication. For the counselor, dreams reveal clients' concerns, resources, and emotional difficulties. For the cognitive therapist, they are indicative of how patients think and feel, and how their minds and schemata are organized. And for behavior therapists, dreams can be used to monitor the progress of efforts to modify their patients' dysfunctions through deconditioning, desensitization, and retraining.

Dreamwork enables gestalt and existential therapists to gain important and otherwise unavailable perspectives on their patients' thinking, whereas the psychopharmacologist can utilize dreams to gain a sense of how a particular medication is affecting his or her patient psychologically. Moreover, group, family, and couples therapists can use dreams to monitor their therapeutic work with their patients and as a means of discovering the hidden effects of their efforts to bring peace and harmony to all concerned. And finally, for the psychodynamically oriented psychotherapist, dreams remain, as Freud so

Introduction

perceptively stated almost 100 years ago, "The royal road to a knowledge of the unconscious activities of the mind" (Freud, 1900, p. 608).

In the years since Freud opened the door to the dynamic study of dreams, clinical and laboratory research investigations have resulted in many remarkable insights into their structure and functions. We now know a great deal about the physiology of dreaming and the emotional ramifications of dream experiences. We have come to appreciate that dreams are special narrative communications that serve human emotional adaptation and reflect the means by which the goals of self-realization, personal and interpersonal harmony, symptom alleviation, and insight can be accomplished. And in a variety of general and not especially disciplined ways, therapists are using dreamwork to enhance the outcome of all types of psychotherapy experiences. For many practitioners, dreamwork is among the most vital means through which they help their patients to achieve sound emotional adaptations and relief from intrapsychic and interpersonal emotional dysfunctions.

Nevertheless, as noted earlier, there are many unresolved problems in the present applications of dreamwork, many of them reflected in the vast differences in how various therapists understand and work with dreams. The present book attempts to clarify this situation and to offer ideas and insights designed to correct and expand current thinking in these areas. Moving from the surface to the depths, I will stress important attributes of dreams that are generally unrecognized and indicate how these features translate into fresh clinical precepts and practices. With respect to format, I have adopted a modified workbook approach in which I present clinical exercises, ask key questions, and provide what I hope are illuminating an-

Introduction

swers. My intention is to engage the reader in an active and participatory search for a comprehensive appreciation of the structure and adaptive functions of dreams as they pertain to the emotional mind and clinical practice.

Summing Up

1. Dreams are heavily condensed communications with both conscious and unconscious meanings.
2. An adaptation-oriented approach to dreams offers a set of new and compelling insights into their structure and functions.
3. Much of the power of dreams to illuminate emotional life and its dysfunctions derives from their storied or narrative qualities.
4. The most powerful level of meaning in dreams is reflected in themes that convey encoded, unconscious responses to emotionally charged incidents and communications, so-called triggering events.
5. Understanding the adaptive functions of dreams and learning how to *trigger decode* their most compelling messages in consideration of adaptation-evoking stimuli provide therapists with a major clinical resource.
6. Broadly stated, this book offers a new understanding of dreams in light of their postulated evolutionary history and current adaptive functions. The interplay among, and ultimate unity of, the emotion-processing mind of the dreamer, his or her environment and its vicissitudes, and the dream experience itself is studied in detail and serves as the basis for formulating fresh ways of doing dreamwork. The ultimate goal is to serve all

Introduction

psychotherapists by enhancing their grasp of the essential nature of dreams as it pertains to both emotional dysfunctions (and health) and the therapeutic process of cure.

PART ONE

Dreams as Psychobiological Communications

CHAPTER ONE

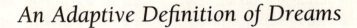

An Adaptive Definition of Dreams

- A sampling of proposed definitions of dreams
- Problems in defining dreams
- The biological roots of psychotherapy and dream communication
- The strong and weak adaptive positions in psychotherapy
- An evolutionary and adaptive definition of dreams

Given the complexity of dreams, there have been many proposals as to how they should be defined. Therefore, we begin here by offering a first approximation of an adaptive definition of dreams, and then exploring issues related to the characterization of the essential features of dreams in order to arrive at a comprehensive definition of the nature and functions of dream communication.

Basically, the communicative approach sees dreams as having messenger rather than processing functions (Langs, 1994, 1995c, 1996b). That is, a dream is understood to be a multilayered reflection of the operations of the emotion-processing mind as it attempts, consciously and deeply unconsciously, to adapt to emotionally charged triggering events.

This means that a dream is at the end point of an adaptive

process, not at the beginning. The important emotional events whose processing is reflected in a dream have already taken place during the dream day (or earlier), and the dream is simultaneously both a direct and an encoded report on the consciously and deeply unconsciously perceived meanings of these evocative events and the patient's responsive attempts to cope. Although efforts at dreamwork and interpretation are the starting point for dream analysis, dreams are at the outcome/response, rather than the origination/stimulus, stage of an adaptive sequence.

Efforts to Define Dreams

The simplest definitions of dreams are descriptive. For example, dreams can be characterized as what humans (and possibly other species) experience when something sensory, usually visual, is imagined during sleep. Some therapists would add that dreams also may take place during the day when a person imagines an event, possibility, or wish. This broadens the definition of dreams to include products of the imagination generated during the waking state, so-called daydreams (Langs, 1995c). This book, however, is confined to nighttime or sleeping-state dreams—those that we commonly mean when we refer to *dreams*.

Phenomenological definitions of dreams are of little or no help in understanding their structure and functions. Amending their definition to indicate that dreams have some bearing on the psychological makeup and emotional life of the dreamer is a rather general and vague addendum, but this refinement does imply that a psychodynamically meaningful definition of dreams must be based on clinical investigations,

An Adaptive Definition of Dreams

with support, perhaps, from laboratory studies. The techniques used and conclusions drawn, however, inevitably will be constrained by the methods employed for collecting dream data and the theory that organizes the resulting observations. Thus, we need to be on the alert for distorting biases and for observations that appear to contradict a particular working definition of dream phenomena—and the theory on which that definition is based.

To bring this point home, even the relatively simple proposition that dreams are relevant to a dreamer's emotional life would be challenged by those who propose an entirely behavioral or laboratory-based neuroscientific, brain-based definition of dreams. Hobson (1988), for example, argues that dreams are psychologically meaningless and merely the result of the firings of pontine nuclei and other brain activities that occur during certain stages of sleep. However, a brain-based definition of dreams confounds *mind* and *brain*, and violates the scientific principle that phenomena at a given level of nature must find their essential explanation and meanings on that level. Thus, it also is necessary to distinguish brain from mind, and to define the psychological aspects of dreams entirely in mental terms. On that basis, given the unique relationship between the brain and the mind, it may be possible to add to the understanding of dreams by exploring their neurophysiological correlates. Nevertheless, the essential definition of dreams must come from the psychological/mental domain.

With this in mind, we can accept a definition of dreams only if it is couched in terms that link them to the emotional life of the dreamer. Indeed, just about every theory of the emotional mind that underlies the practices of psychotherapy and counseling views dreams as meaningful communications that, in one way or another, have a bearing on the emotional problems of the individual who has generated a particular dream.

Problems in Defining Dreams

Some of the difficulties in generating a more specific definition of dreams arise from the treatment of dreams as if they were phenomena that could be isolated for study as detached specimens. Just as we would not define the human heart by isolating it from the body and the individual, we cannot define—or understand—dreams by isolating them from the mind and from the individuals who dream them.

It is, then, vital to forge a definition of dreams that alludes to both the dreamer and his or her environment, a term I use to include both physical and living entities and events (see Introduction and Langs, 1996b). Dreamers are sensitive to both the stabilities and the changes in their environments, including the specific, emotionally charged, adaptation-evoking events or triggers with which they are confronted time and time again. Indeed, a dreamer and his or her environment are a unity that we artificially separate for clinical study, only to reunite them when we are done. Therefore, we will need to define dreams in terms of their essential adaptive functions, albeit with full recognition of their contemporaneous and forward-looking qualities.

There is, however, still more. We also should place dreams in their historical contexts, both collectively and individually. To do so, we must account for the long-term, evolutionary history of dreaming and dreams so as to explain why humans dream at all and to identify their universal adaptive attributes. And we will need to account for the effects of the personal

An Adaptive Definition of Dreams

history of a given dreamer, including the roles of developmental factors and early life experiences, and the chronicle of the relationships and interactions with the people whom a dream concerns—both on its surface and in its disguised depths.

We may conclude, then, that dreams are highly complex phenomena and so their definition will need to be multidimensional and holistic, and should encompass both universal and personal features.

The Biological Roots of Psychotherapy and Dreams

Considering these requisites, there are few, if any, comprehensive definitions of dreams. Although those that have been formulated in terms of cognitive functions, psychodynamics, or interpersonal dynamics have some validity, they fail to capture the essential nature of dreams. What seems to be missing is a sense of the basic nature of dreams as understood in the context of their biological and psychological heritage and functions, especially their role in human adaptation and survival. Thus, as a way of moving toward a more complete definition of dreams, I will make a brief but necessary detour in order to clarify the role of biology in our understanding of the emotion-processing mind and dreams.

In this context, I ask:

Recognizing that psychotherapy is, at its core, a biological science, what is the most fundamental subscience of biology?

The answer may come as a surprise to many psychotherapists because we are unaccustomed to adopting a basic biological view of our field (Slavin & Kriegman, 1992; Langs,

1996a,b). It is, by consensus, the theory of evolution first forged by Darwin and Wallace (Dawkins, 1976; Mayr, 1983; Plotkin, 1994, 1997; Dennett, 1995; Rose, 1998; see Chapter 6). Darwin's theory was later revised into a neo-Darwinian theory (Mayr, 1983; Dawkins, 1976; Slavin & Kriegman, 1992) that, in several forms, stands to this day as the fundamental subtheory of biology (Plotkin, 1994, 1997; Rose, 1998).

In its simplest form, the mechanisms that underlie the evolution of species are currently postulated to involve the favored descent through natural selection of those genes within a species' gene pool that produce bodily and mental organs and functions (phenotypes) that are most advantageous to survival and reproductive success in a particular environment. For humans, evolutionary change also is affected by such factors as mutations, chromosomal crossovers, and other gene-related factors; developmental conditions; coincidental events; intelligence and culture (shared intelligence); and manipulations by humans of their environments. Evolution and the adaptive resources it "forges" are multidetermined processes (Plotkin, 1994, 1997; Rose, 1998).

It follows from these realizations that our understanding of the structure and functions of dreams must be grounded in a full appreciation of the evolutionary history of dream communication and the current role of dreams in emotional adaptation. This dual level of comprehension reflects the existence of two basic components of the theory of evolution. The first deals with the forces and factors—selection pressures and adaptive resources—that have shaped the historical unfolding of species over the billions of years during which living organisms have populated the earth. These efforts are presented as so-called adaptationist programs (Gould & Lewontin, 1979; Mayr, 1983; Tooby & Cosmides, 1990) that trace the history of given features—units of selection (Lewontin,

1979)—of living organisms over extraordinarily long periods. This work and its postulates, however fraught with difficulties (Gould & Lewontin, 1979; Mayr, 1983), constitute the basic theory of evolution, or evolution proper.

The second component of evolutionary theory is focused on the immediate adaptations of an organism in response to the specific conditions of its environment and its vicissitudes. This work involves the development of observation- and data-based theories of the nature, mechanisms, and functions of organismic adaptations as they serve, or fail to serve, both the survival and reproductive success of species and of individual organisms within a given species (Slavin & Kriegman, 1992; Langs, 1995b, 1996a,b). In the emotional domain, these considerations must center on the study of adaptive responses to specific emotionally charged, environmental impingements, including the effects on patients of the interventions of their psychotherapists.

In sum, the evolutionary and adaptive viewpoints are fundamental to biology. It follows as a matter of principle that given that dreams are biological expressions, they, too, must be understood in these terms if we are fully to grasp their significance and meanings. An approach of this kind is certain to illuminate not only the theory and clinical applications that pertain to dream communications, but also the nature of emotional maladaptations and the psychotherapy process.

Weak and Strong Adaptive Viewpoints

The Weak Adaptive Position

By and large, theories of psychotherapy, including psychoanalysis and other dynamic approaches to emotional life, have tended to adopt weak rather than strong adaptive viewpoints.

Thus, although every dynamically oriented theory assumes that patients are attempting to cope emotionally, such theories tend to adopt a very general approach to the problem. They are, on the whole, quite vague as to exactly what it is that patients are trying to cope with; furthermore, adaptation is not the centerpiece of the theory. This way of dealing with adaptation is called *the weak adaptive position* (Langs, 1996a,b, 1998a), and the relative neglect of adaptation is fostered by the reductionistic bent of these theories whereby the goal is to reduce symptoms and their meanings to little more than intrapsychic and personal genetic events.

This strategy began with Freud (1895, 1915/1985; see also Langs, 1996b), who acknowledged that long-term evolutionary factors were relevant to his theories, but whose work in this area was minimal and largely incorrect (Langs, 1996b). Freud (1900) seldom took a close look at the specific adaptive issues facing a dreamer, nor did he seek their reflections in his patients' dreams. Indeed, his most fundamental clinical concept, that of transference, largely precludes adaptive considerations because the patient is seen as projecting fantasies and memories onto the analyst, rather than as adapting, consciously and unconsciously, to the analyst's immediate interventions.

In exploring the nature of dreams, Freud (1900) did, however, introduce the concept of a *day's residues*—the idea that dreams make use of, and sometimes complete the dreamer's work on, emotional issues that were activated on the day of a dream. This proposition speaks for an adaptive orientation, but Freud did not pursue it vigorously. Instead, he mainly saw a day's residues as vehicles that lent shape to dream images and as events that prompted the reactivation of infantile (unconscious) wishes, fantasies, and memories. It was these aroused unconscious constellations that were viewed as the core unconscious contents of dreams, much as they were understood to be the primary unconscious sources of patients' neuroses. This line of thought overshadowed all consideration of immediate adaptive issues.

This is but one of countless examples of how clinical theory strongly affects a therapist's thinking about dreams and their definition, and the meanings that he or she extracts and interprets from their contents.

The Strong Adaptive Position

In contrast, a strong adaptive position places adaptation at the center of our understanding of dreams and their role in emotional life and psychotherapy (Langs, 1996a,b). Dreams are seen as part of a dreamer's efforts to adapt both consciously and unconsciously to immediate, quite specific, emotionally charged stimuli—so-called triggering events—that occur during the dream day, or, in some cases, one or more days before that (Langs, 1988, 1994). This approach to dreams finds considerable support in clinical observations developed from the perspective of the adaptational–interactional or communicative approach to dynamic psychotherapy on which much of this book is based (Smith, 1991, 1998; Langs, 1992a; see Chapter 4). It also finds backing theoretically in the realization that adaptation to environmental events is the fundamental task and function of all organisms, including humans.

The principle that conceptions related to evolution and adaptation are the basis for the fundamental subtheory of biology has wider implications for our efforts to comprehend the functions and meanings of dreams. It implies that the definition and ideas we develop regarding the structure and functions of dreams must not contradict the precepts of evolutionary theory; that is, a higher-level theory must be consonant with, and cannot violate, the propositions of more basic theories.

A cogent example of the ramifications of this proposal is seen in the emphasis in psychoanalysis on the etiological power of unconscious fantasies and memories as factors in neurosogenesis. Both the intrapsychic and interpersonal versions of this line of thought are based on weak adaptive positions. The stress on internal dynamics overlooks or downplays the crucial role played by the dreamer's adaptations to his or her external environment and its most immediate changes or triggers. This thinking precludes the development of a strong adaptive position that is in keeping with Darwinian principles (Langs, 1995b, 1996a,b). In other words, the focus on unconscious fantasy, while of some merit, serves defensively to bypass the more compelling role of unconscious perception in human emotional life and in the production of dreams (Langs, 1992b).

The adaptation-oriented theory of evolution is unswerving in its proposition that adaptations to external or environmental events are the primary issues for all living organisms. This principle appears to apply to humans despite their rich and complex inner mental lives, which are, first and foremost, aspects of adaptive responses to external events, and only secondarily, adaptive issues in their own right.

The adaptive approach to the emotional mind and dreams has been relatively neglected by the various theories of psychotherapy. In recent years, however, a field of evolutionary psychoanalysis has been developing, with efforts to forge broad evolutionary perspectives on such subjects as human bonding and emotionally meaningful relatedness (Slavin & Kriegman, 1992), the Oedipus complex (Badcock, 1990a,b), the problem of altruism (Badcock, 1986), psychological defenses and the mechanism of repression (Nesse, 1990b; Lloyd, 1990; Nesse

An Adaptive Definition of Dreams

& Lloyd, 1992), the experience of emotions and affects (Nesse, 1990a), and psychoanalysis in general (Badcock, 1994).

These researchers have shown that psychological phenomena and mental mechanisms, such as those pertaining to dreams, function adaptively and have evolutionary histories that are comparable to those of bodily organs and processes (Tooby & Cosmides, 1990). Their work provides strong support for the position that emotion-related phenomena and their meanings are not simply matters of hermeneutics, but are part of the biology and biological psychology of human beings. Supplemented by recent studies of adaptation and the evolution of adaptive mental functions carried out from the vantage point of the communicative approach (Langs, 1996a,b; see Chapters 4 and 6), these endeavors are a prelude to a comprehensive, adaptation-oriented definition of dreams.

A Comprehensive Definition of Dreams

In keeping with the two components of the theory of evolution—the historical and the contemporary, a satisfactory and comprehensive definition of dreams as psychobiological phenomena also will have two constituents (Langs, 1996b). The first component pertains to evolution proper and is historical in nature. It calls for a definition of dreams in terms of the distal or ultimate causal factors that account for why dreams exist in humans and how they serve to enhance both survival and reproductive success. The second component calls for a proximate, functional, or mechanistic definition, one that explains what dreams do and how they operate psychologically. In substance, this would translate into a definition of dreams in terms of their *active adaptive functions*. Both aspects of the adaptation-oriented definitions of dreams have the potential to offer fresh perspectives on, and insights into, the structure, functions, and meanings of dreams.

As for an all-encompassing definition, which will be used as a basis for exploring the ways in which dreams contribute to and illuminate human emotional adaptations and the psychotherapy experience, the following is proposed.

Their *proximal definition* sees dreams as phenomena that occur in the sleeping state in the form of sensory images that serve as part of human efforts to adapt to specific, complex, currently active, emotionally charged triggering events. Dreams function as multilayered communicative vehicles that embody both direct and encoded meanings that are reflections of the conscious and deep unconscious experiences and adaptive processing efforts of the emotion-processing mind.

Their *distal definition* sees dreams as having evolved as part of imagistic, and then language-based, human efforts to cope over the past half-million years with the ever-increasing intensification of stressful, traumatic, and potentially disruptive emotionally charged environmental events. This mounting overload of emotional challenges began to overtax the coping capabilities of the hominid mind, thereby endangering the survival of the species. By means of natural selection, advantageous mental resources—changes in the design of the emotion-processing mind—were favorably reproduced.

As part of these developments, which have mostly unfolded in the relatively short span of the last 150,000 years or so, dreams have played a role in the trade-off between faithful representations of painful reality events and the deceptive falsification of the meanings of these events. Functioning as messengers, and embodying conscious and, especially, deep unconscious experiences and adaptive inclinations, dreams have served as compromise formations that express, yet fail to express (i.e., that disguise or encode), the true nature of emotionally charged realities.

In this respect, dreams reflect the evolved basic defensive design of the emotion-processing mind and its natural tendency to register unconsciously and then encode expressively the anxiety-provoking meanings of traumatic events. This basic use of denial and repressive mechanisms appears to have evolved to spare the cognitive mind potentially disruptive emotionally charged inputs so that humans can function without undue disruption (Langs, 1996b, 1997; see Chapter 6). Dreams are, then, part of an evolved adaptive solution to emotional overload that has entailed considerable cost through a significant loss, or reduction, in our knowledge of many of the most critical aspects of emotionally charged human experiences.

These adaptive definitions of dreams take us to the heart of the structure, functions, and meanings of dreams. They also indicate that as encoded messages, dreams have the potential to contribute to deep insight and emotional healing, but can do so only when they are properly decoded and interpreted.

Summing Up

1. Dreams are most meaningfully defined within an adaptive framework.
2. Psychoanalysis (and psychotherapy) is best understood as a subscience of biology.
   a. The theory of evolution is the fundamental subscience of biology.
   b. Evolutionary theory deals with both distal, or historical, causes (evolution proper) and proximal

DREAMS AND EMOTIONAL ADAPTATION

causes (current adaptations and their immediate provocations).

c. *Dreamwork*, the theoretical understanding of, and clinical work with, dreams, should be developed with a full appreciation for, and within the constraints posed by, the findings of evolutionary biology and evolutionary psychoanalysis.

3. The weak adaptive position, which is characteristic of most present-day psychotherapies, considers adaptation in broad, global terms that are far too ill defined to meaningfully describe the structure and functions of the emotional mind and its adaptive successes and failures—symptomatic maladaptations.

4. The communicative approach, on which this book is based, takes into account both emotionally charged, environmental events (stimuli or triggers) and inner resources and responses.

a. It examines in detail the nature and structure of emotionally charged, adaptation-evoking stimuli or triggering events.

b. It also carefully scrutinizes and explores patients' conscious and unconscious adaptive responses to these triggers.

5. This meticulous examination of both sides of emotional adaptations—their triggers and their inner basis, a fundamental unity—facilitates an understanding of the architecture of the emotion-processing mind and its adaptive capabilities and preferences. This approach has led to an unprecedented, deep understanding of emotional life, dreams, and the process of psychotherapy.

6. The adaptation-oriented definition of dreams sees them:

An Adaptive Definition of Dreams

    a.   Distally and historically, as the evolved outcome of imagistic and language-based efforts to cope with an escalating load of emotionally charged inputs that have confronted evolving hominids.

    b.   Proximally, as serving immediate emotional adaptation by functioning as messengers that convey both conscious and unconscious communicative and mental responses to emotionally charged triggering events.

7.   All in all, dreams are an excellent means of understanding and interpreting the adaptive issues and individual responses that determine the vicissitudes of the emotional lives of psychotherapy patients.

CHAPTER TWO

Dreams and Nondynamic Theories of the Mind

- Dreams as part of the interaction between (the mind of) a dreamer and his or her environment
- Exploring approaches to dreams by various schools of psychotherapy in light of their models of the mind
- The six levels on which emotional healing and the understanding of dreams are grounded
- The behavioral and cognitive approaches to dreamwork

To fully understand the nature and function of dreams, we need to know both parts of an adaptive whole: the evocative stimuli or triggers that set off dream responses and the dreamers who are responding to these triggering events. Dreams mediate between environmental conditions and the mind of the dreamer. It follows, then, that we need to appreciate the basic status of the environment, both settings and people, and the nature of immediate environmental events, as well as the psychological and emotional history and current state of the individual who is trying to cope with these emotionally charged events, in part by having a dream.

Thus, we could begin our exploration of dreams by looking at either the triggers that evoke dreams or the minds of the dreamers who report them. In principle, each choice requires an understanding of the other half of the picture. This is necessary because, although reality events have inherent meanings, those meanings to which a given dreamer selectively responds depend on the dreamer's inner mental state and life history. Reality and inner experience are relatively autonomous and yet inseparably interdependent.

Models of the Emotional Mind

Because the theories of psychotherapy have had far more to say about dreamers than about their adaptation-evoking triggers, we begin by examining the mind of the dreamer to learn how dreams are created. And to do this in an informative manner, we must also appreciate how a given theory and its model of the emotional mind affect its understanding of dreamers and their dreams. Adopted by Freud (1900) in his landmark book on the interpretation of dreams, this approach will enable us to see from the outset how a theory of the mind shapes both the selection of clinical observations and their interpretation—and the dreamwork carried out by its practitioners. The many different approaches to dreamwork are a result of the existence of many different theories and models of the mind in current psychotherapy.

Because model making, which plays a vital role in all of the other sciences, is not stressed in psychotherapy, many therapists work with dreams intuitively, without an explicit picture of the workings of the human mind. This situation allows for many loosely defined, and sometimes arbitrary, efforts at dreamwork that go unchallenged because of an absence of definitive criteria for the validation of the ensuing dream interpretations. And while some of this work may be credible, because of the absence of confirmatory indicators, it is impossible to assess its effects. Given that dreamwork has a great impact on both patients and therapists, we are in serious need of a definitive means of deciding on the validity, power, and effectiveness of dream explorations and interpretations of all types.

Although the mind is an enormously complicated entity, the prevailing, relatively simple models of the emotional mind put much of that complexity aside. Simplified views of dreams allow for easy interpretation, but create blind spots that often have dire consequences for all concerned. Models that permit simple extractions of meanings from the surface or manifest contents of dreams, for example, overlook the powerful unconscious experiences and meanings that are being processed by the emotional mind and encoded in these same dreams, along with their rather compelling consequences. Nevertheless, each model of the mind, including those that bypass the mind entirely, as in behaviorism, has some credibility, whatever its limitations or flaws.

Levels of Intervention

To orient us in exploring the interplay between models of the mind and dreamwork, it is helpful to realize that attempts to understand and ameliorate emotional maladaptations can be carried out on several different levels of human functioning and experience. Each level will have a characteristic approach to working with dreams.

In what ways or at what levels can emotional maladaptations be treated?

The hierarchy of possible therapeutic interventions may be ranked in terms of the complexity of the effort and its under-

Dreams and Nondynamic Theories of the Mind

lying theory and model of the mind, beginning with the simplest, nonmental approaches. Thus, a therapist may intervene with a patient at the following levels:

1. *The brain substrate* of the mind and of emotional behavior—pharmacological or drug treatments.
2. *Behavioral*—treatment of symptoms and behavior dysfunctions directly without psychological or mind-oriented interventions.
3. *Experiential*—manifest or direct approaches to the human condition and emotional experience, such as the existential and phenomenological forms of therapy that stress clarifications of experiencing and being.
4. *Cognitive*—manifest or direct approaches to patients' modes of thinking, beliefs, moods, affects, values, and the like.
5. *Superficial unconscious*—therapeutic work with manifest contents and extractions of their evident but unrealized implications, and with symbolic meanings that are isolated from ongoing adaptive issues, as well as explorations of disguised themes whose meanings are relatively transparent and easily formulated.
6. *Deep unconscious*—therapeutic work that decodes themes in light of their adaptation-evoking triggering events, thereby revealing the deep unconscious perceptions and reactions to these perceptions that unconsciously motivate emotional maladaptations.

Each of these levels of intervention has advantages and disadvantages with respect to its applied modes of therapy. Each configures an approach to dreamwork; each can bring a measure of relief to patients, although, in many cases, without meaningful insight; and each has its limitations and cost.

A Dream Specimen

Before turning to the models of the mind and the dreamwork they engender, consider a clinical vignette.*

Edna Wile, a 29-year-old, phobic patient who was in therapy with John Thorpe, began a session six months into her treatment with the following dream.

> She is in the bedroom of an expensive apartment with a man with a mustache, whom she doesn't recognize. A tall free-form glass statue stands in one corner of the room; it has a long, oblong shape. The man is being seductive. He tries to touch Ms. Wile's breasts and to force her to get into bed with him, but she pushes him off and throws him to the floor.

We have here a dream specimen that is offered without associations or a description of the dreamer and her psychotherapy—and whatever additional supplementary information we might want to have. As we explore the models of the mind, this material will be used for purposes of illustration.

---

*The vignettes in this book are fictitious. They are offered as illustrations and are faithful to clinical experience. The reader is encouraged to turn to his or her own clinical work to verify and extend the insights and principles offered here.

Dreams and Nondynamic Theories of the Mind

Two Misguided Models

The Mind as a User of Universal Symbols

There are at least two models of the mind that we, as psychotherapists, should dispose of because they are of little emotional import and cannot form the basis for meaningful or effective dreamwork. The first of these models posits an emotional mind that operates solely in terms of universal meanings and inherited representational tendencies: the symbolic approach.

There is considerable evidence for the existence of universal symbols, but their exclusive use in working with dreams creates a highly impersonal and only weakly, if at all, adaptive form of dreamwork that leaves little or no room for individual experiences and tendencies. It is, in some hands, a misrepresentation of the Jungian theory of dreams, which actually argues for the individual use of symbols and for both a universal or archetypical and a personal level of meaning to dream images (Maidenbaum, 1998; see Chapter 3). Practitioners of the dreamwork based on the model of the mind as a symbol maker draw on lists of universal symbols that are said to reveal to dreamers the nature of their emotional issues and thinking.

The oblong statue in Ms. Wile's dream, for example, would be said to represent a phallus. On this basis, it might be suggested that she was dealing with her masculine self or identity, or with penis envy, or with heterosexuality. These speculations are without substantiation and are so broad and general as to be of little importance despite their small measure of possibility. This is a nondynamic, static, dehumanizing approach to dreams that has little place in a psychotherapy process.

The identification of universal representational elements in dreams offers the least compelling level of meaning that can be derived from dream communications. Nevertheless, these propositions are popular because they are simple, formulistic, remote, yet alluring, and above all, not especially cogent to the immediate, disturbing emotional issues of a dreamer. As we shall see, humans are strongly inclined to accept deceptive, misleading, and superficial ideas about their dreams and emotional lives—they have a highly defensive orientation in the emotional realm (Langs, 1996b, 1997).

The Mind as Brain
A second misleading approach to the emotional mind has some validity on its own level, but is a disservice to efforts to comprehend the most compelling psychological meanings of dreams. It is based on a model that sees the mind as the brain, and it results in attempts to define the properties of the mind of a dreamer in neuroscientific terms (e.g., Hobson, 1988).

This approach would have little to say about the content of Ms. Wile's dream, but instead would turn to brain measurements for its commentary. Since the goal of this book is to explore the mental realm and psychological adaptations, the brain will not be included in the following discussions. While neurological correlates to mental events are of interest and may be informative, and may in time provide unforeseen insights into our understanding of the psychology of dreams, at present they have little relevance to clinical practice and the applications of dreamwork.

The Behavioral Model of the Mind

The behavioral model of the mind is based on theories of learning and conditioning, and it leads to therapeutic efforts

Dreams and Nondynamic Theories of the Mind

designed to directly modify maladaptive or dysfunctional behaviors. In this approach, the mind is viewed as a collection of innate, conditioned, and learned responses. Mental events per se are seldom considered. Instead, the focus is on behavior, a term that includes such symptoms as habit disorders, phobias, obsessions, and anxiety attacks. While behavior therapists attempt to modify these behaviors through direct interventions, such as deconditioning, desensitization, and relearning methods, the mind can play an indirect role in this work because communications, such as dreams, can be used to monitor the progress of these therapeutic efforts.

To return to Ms. Wile's dream, what can be said of it from the perspective of behaviorism and what might a possible behavioral scenario pertaining to her dream imagery look like?

There are two main reasons why these questions are difficult to answer. First, behaviorists do not examine mental events and they have little to say about psychological phenomena. Second, we are severely limited in establishing any level of understanding regarding Ms. Wile's dream because we know nothing about her life history, current and past environments, psychotherapy, and emotional issues. Trying to work with an isolated dream is mostly guesswork.

Still, to speculate, it might be the case that Ms. Wile has had difficulties in relating to men. She may have been undergoing deconditioning exercises to modify her aversive responses to them. If so, the dream suggests that these efforts have not been especially effective; she still is pushing men away. Another possibility is that Ms. Wile's behavior actually has changed through relearning efforts. If this is the case, the dream might indicate that her underlying conflicts with men have not been altered even though her behavior has changed. A combined study of Ms. Wile's behaviors and her dreams is the best possible approach on this level.

Behavior therapists who try to make use of dreams will, as a rule, devote their attention to manifest dream contents and their evident implications. The surface of this patient's dream, for example, reveals a conflict with a man, a picture of him as sexually assaultive, and her rejecting, defensive response. These are manifest themes and they are used as such by behavior therapists—and by most other types of psychotherapists, as well.

The Cognitive Model

There are many cognitive models of the mind. Their focus is on cognition, the means by which we know and communicate about the world around us and through which we mentally process the stimuli emanating from that world. Cognitive models of the mind stress information processing and view the mind as composed of belief systems, values, goals, schemata (structures of information organized around a particular aspect of emotional life), and the like. Emotional symptoms are understood to be the result of faulty belief systems and schemata, and they are treated by techniques that promote changes in thought patterns, as seen, for example, with interventions designed to lead to cognitive restructuring (Stein, 1997).

These models of the mind postulate both conscious and unconscious components to cognitive processing and a patient's thought patterns, schemata, and belief systems. The unconscious aspects of these contents and processes can be brought into awareness through direct extractions and inferences that lead to the conscious recognition of an identified thought pattern, belief system, or self-image. The unconscious mind as defined in the cognitive approach is a relatively fixed domain of internal inclinations and thought systems that are partly innate and partly learned; that is, created through experience. This latter proviso reflects an ill-defined, weak adaptive approach.

There is, then, a sense that a patient's thinking and its effects on his or her mood and symptoms can be modified without significant knowledge of his or her conflicts, environment, or critical adaptation-evoking triggers. There also is a tendency to think of the mind in terms of fixed modules open to structural change, rather than as modules that are actively interacting with and affected by the environment.

Work with dreams is not a major feature of cognitive therapies (for an exception, see Lakoff, 1997, and for a combined cognitive and psychodynamic approach, see Haskell, 1989). Nevertheless, dreams can be used to gauge a patient's cognitive attitudes and processes, and to examine the status of a patient's mental schemata. And in a manner similar to that used by behavior therapists, dreams also can be used to evaluate the progress of efforts at cognitive restructuring.

Can we identify some of the possible ways in which Ms. Wile's dream may reflect her values, beliefs, expectancies, and schemata?

Ms. Wile may have a belief system that sees men as inappropriately seductive, unduly aggressive, and exploitative, and a schema pertaining to relationships with men that organizes and colors her experiences with them as assaultive and unfeeling. If she were in a cognitive therapy that was designed to modify these beliefs and this schema, the dream would suggest that this work had not as yet been successful.

In a manner similar to the behavioral approach, cognitive therapists work with the surface meanings of dreams and define their implications according to cognitive theory. Most cognitive models of the mind acknowledge mental operations that take place without awareness. Although they conceive of split-off mental contents, they make only limited and highly intellectualized use of such psychodynamic concepts as repression and denial and intrapsychic and interpersonal conflict. They also view communication largely in manifest and conscious terms, and fail to appreciate many of the intricacies of unconscious experience, communication, and dynamic information processing.

All in all, the cognitive models of the mind promote relatively nondynamic, manifest content approaches to dreams that only minimally consider issues of emotional adaptation. Meanings are extracted directly from dreams and used for perspectives regarding cognitive issues and treatment techniques. Given the relative simplicity of these efforts, there is little or no need for associations to dreams and little sense of the vast world of human experience that lies beyond the surface of the emotional mind and the dreams it creates. The achievement of easily available insights is possible, but the vast world of active deep unconscious experience goes untapped—and unacknowledged.

Summing Up

1. Dreams are interactionally based communications and are part of the interplay between the mind of a dreamer and the stabilities and instabilities in his or her environment.
2. However well or poorly defined, each approach to psychotherapy has a model of the emotional mind and of cure, as well as a method of dreamwork.
3. The main levels at which emotional dysfunctions can be understood and modified are the brain, behavior,

Dreams and Nondynamic Theories of the Mind

conscious experience, cognition or thinking, superficial unconscious, and deep unconscious.

4. The goal of the behavioral approach to emotionally based maladaptations is directly to modify the patient's symptoms and interpersonal difficulties.

   a. For this approach, dreams can be used to monitor the status of, and basis for, a patient's behavioral changes.

   b. As a rule, the therapist's focus is on the implications of the patient's manifest dream images, often without accompanying associations to the dream's elements.

5. The cognitive approach to emotionally based maladaptations is based on theories of how humans know, think about, and respond to their environments.

   a. With its focus on inner thoughts and attitudes, the dreamwork used with this approach tends to be surface oriented; at times, the surface meanings of associations to dream elements are also explored.

   b. Dreamwork is used to understand and monitor the ways in which patients think about the world and themselves, and how these attitudes affect their emotional maladaptations.

CHAPTER THREE

Dreams and Psychodynamic Models of the Mind

- The psychodynamic models of the mind and dreamwork developed by Freud and Jung
- Freud's two models of the mind: the topographic (unconscious, preconscious, conscious) and the structural (ego, id, and superego)
- Jung's model of two compensatory systems of the mind and dreamwork that deals with universal archetypes and individual conflicts
- Assets and liabilities of the dreamwork generated by these psychodynamic models of the mind

Psychodynamic models of the mind, and the dreamwork they support, attempt to account for the full range of human emotional experience, including both the conscious and unconscious meanings of dreams. Nevertheless, the currently accepted dynamic models of the mind are incomplete and the dreamwork they engender is more unrevealing than revealing, more a matter of defense and deception than of deep insight (Langs, 1992b,c, 1995b, 1996b).

The proposal that psychodynamically oriented dreamwork has notable limitations can be best appreciated in the context of a relevant perspective. Both models of the mind and the dreamwork they promote tend to be internally consistent and, as defined by the model, complete. That is, a psychological model or theory is like a lens through which the emotional

Dreams and Psychodynamic Models of the Mind

world is viewed. The lens is focused on those aspects of that world that it has been designed to incorporate selectively and the resultant observations are then subjected to analysis.

Freudian, Jungian, and other psychodynamics lenses are theorized to be all encompassing. Nevertheless, a higher-power or wider lens—and theory—would show that this is not the case. The histories of science and biology indicate that such an advance is inevitable. Progress made within a particular theory can widen the range of its lens, and also may reveal that the lens is out of focus in some respects. But only the emergence of a new paradigm with a wider or different lens can justify basic revisions in an accepted theory and its dreamwork applications (Kuhn, 1962; Raney, 1984).

Within a given paradigm, existing lenses are more or less supported for long periods. It takes years of confrontation with major unsolved puzzles—observations that a theory cannot account for (Kuhn, 1962)—before this package of model, theory, and lens is overhauled, revised, and fashioned into a new paradigm. Doing so is especially problematic in psychotherapy because it is not a formal science that can relatively incisively expose inaccurate precepts. The field also suffers strongly from the human tendency to sustain, however false, shared belief systems and the inclination to accept or overlook unsolved puzzles and erroneous formulations. Thus, the discovery of errors and limitations and the recognition of dire signs that change is needed are exceedingly slow to come about. With the likely exception of the communicative approach, there has been no major paradigm shift in the history of dynamic psychotherapies (Raney, 1984; Langs, 1992b).

Similar considerations apply to the dream theories and dreamwork that evolve from a given model of the mind. In terms of the existing psychodynamic models, to their adherents, the understanding of dreams appears to be complete and satisfying. The fact that competing psychodynamic models challenge each other has little impact because practitioners who utilize a given model are not receptive to criticisms from those who use competing theories and models. Freudian therapists, for example, give little credence to Jungian thinking, whereas Jungian therapists basically object to what they see as the very constricted Freudian approaches. However, psychotherapists have not as yet put into place a rigorous means of testing the validity of their clinical precepts and techniques. There is a laissez-faire attitude toward dreamwork that seems inappropriate when seeking scientific truths and intervening in the lives of humans.

In essence, the state of the field of psychotherapy allows for the wide range of approaches to dreamwork that are explored here. Each has a measure of internal consistency and seeming validity within the realm defined by its lens and model of the mind. The main problem lies in the absence of an overarching means of testing the truth value, validity, relevance, power, utility, therapeutic potential, effects, and underlying basis of the results of a given effort at dreamwork. Indeed, the lack of a means of falsifiability creates an undisciplined and uncertain situation.

With these perspectives in view, we turn to the prevailing psychoanalytically oriented models of the mind. These models, and the dreamwork they foster, undertake to move beyond behavioral and cognitive efforts by attempting to take into account the psychodynamic aspects of unconscious experience, relatedness, interaction, and conflict. The stress is on unconscious contents and processes, whether interpersonally or intrapsychically conceptualized.

The First Psychoanalytic Model of the Mind

Two early psychodynamic models of the mind were forged by Freud (1900, 1923), and modified to some extent by later psychoanalytic theorists (Langs, 1998a). A third model was offered by Jung (1974). The Freudian models are relatively well defined, whereas although the Jungian model has features that were overlooked by Freud, it is rather vaguely conceived. As noted, in principle, the more uncertain the model of the mind, the looser is the resultant dreamwork and the greater is the therapist's use of ill-defined formulations and interpretations.

Freud's (1900) first model of the mind was the *topographic* model. The model was not, however, all encompassing with respect to the mind, but restricted itself to the processing of emotionally charged inputs. Thus, Freud was dealing with the emotional mind, or what I call the emotion-processing mind (Langs, 1995a).

Freud postulated the existence of three interconnected mental systems, viewed mainly as containers for mental contents: unconscious (UCS), preconscious (PCS), and conscious (CS). The basic division was between the UCS and CS, and the PCS was seen as the gateway to the CS system. The UCS was the locale of forbidden mental contents: memories and fantasies, mainly sexual and incestuous in nature. The CS was a container for only those mental contents that are acceptable to awareness (and the individual). Thus, unacceptable UCS mental contents could enter the CS only in disguised form: censorships or defenses at the UCS-PCS and PCS-CS borders ensured that camouflage would be invoked before a wish or fantasy reached awareness.

Contents within the UCS and CS also had distinctive attributes and were processed differently. For example, UCS contents, mainly forbidden sexual wishes and memories, were said to seek blind discharge without regard for reality, and the energies of the UCS were thought of as mobile cathexes in that their representations could be easily transformed; that is, disguised, displaced, and condensed. In contrast, the CS was seen to operate with bound cathexes in that its contents were fixed and not transformable, and also the system was in touch with reality.

In this model, the emotional mind was considered, to some extent, a processor of information and meaning; that is, as dealing with events or stimuli—inputs—that, in all cases, were said to be initially perceived and registered consciously (CS). (Despite knowledge of the phenomenon, Freud never included unconscious perception in his models of the mind and dream formation.) Following conscious registration, those contents that were forbidden were sent to the UCS, from which they moved through a series of disguise-invoking censors to the PCS and, once there, quite readily to the CS. This implicitly recognized processing capability of the emotional mind was not developed further in the theory and dreamwork that Freud established on the basis of this model.

As it pertains to dreams, the UCS was seen as a reservoir for the forbidden sexual and incestuous wishes that are subject to censorship and distortion in order to go through the PCS to the CS, where they attract the hypercathexes of attention and reach awareness, albeit in disguised form. Therefore, dreams were viewed primarily as the disguised expression of unconscious wishes, fantasies, and memories that are activated by a day's residues, or unfinished events from the dream day.

The goal of dreamwork was to unmask the disguised dream and disclose *the latent contents* camouflaged in the manifest or surface dream images—and thereby to interpret the patient's repressed, unconscious fantasies and memories. It was postulated that these wishes are the source of the intrapsychic conflicts that motivate and lie beneath neurotic symptoms. The main mental conflict is between the UCS wish and the CS conscience, with the defenses of the censorships serving as the mediators of the struggle.

As for the psychological mechanisms of disguise, Freud (1900) ingeniously identified *displacement* and *symbolization* (representing one thing by another) as the basic means by which raw UCS wishes are transformed into disguised manifest dream images. These mechanisms were said to operate in the service of the defense of *repression*—as a way to keep forbidden UCS wishes from entering the CS system undisguised. To this basic repertoire, Freud added *condensation* (using a single dream image to disguise and represent multiple unconscious wishes), concerns for representability, and secondary revision (making the manifest dream images somewhat sensible to the conscious mind). The dreamwork derived from this model operated to undo the effects of these mental mechanisms so as to unmask the conflicts they defended against and disguised, including the underlying sexual wishes. Once this was done, the unconscious connections between these conflicts and a patient's symptoms were identified and worked through.

Overall, the mind was viewed as a series of systems that contain and modify forbidden sexual wishes (aggressive wishes were considered in a later model; Freud, 1923), which then might find CS expression in disguised form—as dream images, symptoms, and/or behaviors. The focus of the dreamwork was on the underlying or latent dream contents, and the manifest dream (the dream as dreamed) was seen essentially as a disguised vehicle for these critical latent, unconscious contents.

To this day, there are many Freudian analysts and therapists who carry out dreamwork on the basis of this early Freudian model. Stress is placed on unconscious sexual wishes and conflicts, and dream images are mined for disguised expressions of these wishes and associated memories, which are then interpreted to the patient and connected with his or her symptomatic difficulties. Much of this work involves exploring the seemingly unconscious implications of manifest themes, and it is explicated in terms of a generalized, weak adaptive position. Many of these latent contents are unmasked in the context of the patient's relationship with his or her therapist or analyst; that is, in terms of the so-called transference relationship. Some therapists add explorations of latent aggressive wishes to this mix, and they are convinced of the therapeutic efficacy of the illumination of these repressed UCS wishes and memories, whether sexual or aggressive. The details of such dreamwork will become clear in Part II, when we consider specific ways of interpreting dreams.

Using this model of the mind, how would you fashion a possible interpretation of Edna Wile's dream, presented in Chapter 2?

The manifest dream can be interpreted as reflecting Ms. Wile's latent dream wish for a phallus (disguised, yet represented by the oblong statue) and as conveying a repudiated unconscious masochistic rape fantasy with incestuous roots (disguised via the interaction with the man).

The patient's UCS incestuous wishes for her father, and memories associated with these wishes, are camouflaged in the image of the stranger, and are further defended against by displacing (and projecting) the wishes onto him; it is not Ms. Wile who wishes to have sex with her father or her therapist "in the transference," but her disguised father/therapist who wishes to have sex with her. In addition, the image in which

Dreams and Psychodynamic Models of the Mind

Ms. Wile pushes off the attacker suggests a CS system repudiation of this wish; in this model, the conscience was located in the CS system, a feature that led to the model's being dropped because of evidence of patients' UCS guilt (see below).

We can see here how a theory and its model of the mind constrain and virtually dictate the nature of the dreamwork and a therapist's interpretations. It also is evident that extractions from manifest dream images are used in this approach to define purported unconscious contents (a method that I later will contrast with that of trigger decoding, in which an image is decoded in light of the emotionally charged event that evoked it). Were Ms. Wile to agree with the intervention or recover a sexual memory of her father, the interpretation would be seen as confirmed. Were she to object to the interpretation, she would be seen as being defensive and resistant because of the anxieties caused by her repressed incestuous wishes.

Undoubtedly, unconscious sexual and aggressive wishes toward the father exist in every young girl and woman, and they are indeed displaced onto other men, including therapists, and are the source of considerable unconscious conflict. Nevertheless, interpreting such wishes in isolation and without reference to the events that evoked them involves overly intellectualized speculations that diminish the power and relevance of these interpretations as they relate to a patient's emotional life and issues.

With all this said, therapists nevertheless are well advised to be wary of their personal investment in their manner of conducting dreamwork. They also must recognize the need for a reliable method of validating its every aspect. There is a general inclination to avoid looking at alternative possibilities of meaning or interpretation because they tend to be precluded by the model of the mind a therapist is using. This lack of flexibility creates blind spots with respect to many pertinent emotional issues—most of them involving efforts to adapt to emotionally charged, environmental events and their meanings as experienced via unconscious perception. Given that such perceptions consistently involve valid appraisals of therapists' interventions (Langs, 1992a,b, 1993), it seems likely that whatever the truth value of dream-based interpretations derived from this or the other prevailing psychoanalytic models, these interventions also serve analysts as vehicles of self-deception and the deception of patients. They are a theory-sanctioned means of invoking defensive denial with regard to a therapist's own contributions to a patient's dream experiences and emotional state, especially when that state is dysfunctional.

This point was developed several decades ago by Little (1951) and Szasz (1962) in connection with transference interpretations that they saw as defensively structured in a similar manner: in describing a patient's reaction to the therapist as a transference-based distortion, the therapist is exonerated from any significant contribution to the patient's experience. Recent interpersonally oriented efforts to rectify the situation by acknowledging analysts' ill-defined and consciously formulated evocative behaviors vis-à-vis their patients have done little to correct this fundamental error. Based on a weak adaptive position (Langs, 1992b, 1998a), they retain the denial of the specific unconscious meanings and effects of therapists' moment-to-moment interventions as unconsciously perceived by their patients.

Freud, as noted, eventually questioned the accuracy of his initial model of the mind (see Freud, 1923). He discovered two major unsolved puzzles that motivated him to revise the model: first, the recognition of patients' unconscious guilt (i.e.,

Dreams and Psychodynamic Models of the Mind

unconscious needs for punishment), a finding that ran counter to his placement of the conscience in the system CS; and second, the realization that resistances and defenses, such as patients' objections to interpretations Freud believed to be valid, also were often unconscious (UCS) (i.e., the patient was not aware that he or she was resisting). This observation implied the existence of UCS system defenses, yet he had placed defenses in the CS system.

Freud's fundamental clinical theory posited that *intrapsychic conflict* is the primary source of neuroses. His model of the mind had been designed to define the nature of these conflicts and had located them as a struggle between the UCS and CS. Freud thus saw himself as faced with a choice: he had to either give up his conflict theory or abandon his model of the mind. Unfortunately, he did not envision a third alternative whereby he could have revised both conflict theory and his information-processing model of the mind in a way that would render them compatible and highly serviceable. Had he done so, he would have arrived at a solution that would have been quite close to that developed through the communicative approach (Langs, 1992a,b; see Chapter 4).

As is generally known, Freud decided to give up his topographic model of the mind and proposed a dramatically different model in its place. In so doing, he abandoned the concept of conscious and unconscious mental systems, and replaced them with a trio of systems (ego, id, and superego), each of which had an unconscious component. The term *unconscious* lost its systemic meaning and was reduced to a quality of mental contents (and, to some extent, mental operations), which were either conscious or unconscious— within awareness or not. This change led to a degradation of the concept of an unconscious domain, the hallmark of psychoanalysis. It also involved a critical loss of understanding of the emotional mind as a system that processes or adapts to emotionally charged events and their meanings (Langs, 1992b).

The Second Freudian Model

The second psychodynamic model of the mind is known as the *structural model* (Freud, 1923; Arlow & Brenner, 1964). The model involves the now-familiar picture of a tripartite mind composed of three interconnected systems: ego, id, and superego. In essence, the ego carries out the executive functions and defenses of the mind, and mediates the interactions between the self and the external world; the id is the source of instinctual drives, sexual and aggressive; and the superego accounts for the conscience, morals, ideals, and self-regulation.

Whereas the defining feature of the systems of the topographic model was that of conscious versus unconscious contents, the defining feature of the structural model is that of function. Each of the structural systems is said to have conscious and unconscious features, so that *conscious* and *unconscious* became terms that were, as noted, reduced to little more than qualities of contents and functions.

The structural model is a static model of the mind, a view that stresses collections of functions and defines conflict largely in terms of forbidden id wishes and impulses as opposed by superego constraints. This ever-present conflict is mediated by the ego, which deals with the problem by activating its defenses. Of these defenses, repression is the most basic, although it is supported by such subsidiary defenses as projection, undoing, reaction formation, isolation, and denial.

According to the structural model of the mind, dreams are

representations of the capacities and inclinations of the three systems of the mind. With stress again placed on latent contents, dreams are understood to reflect conscious and unconscious intrapsychic conflicts aroused by incestuous and/or aggressive id wishes that evoke superego condemnations and prompt the ego to mobilize its defenses so as to deal with the conflict. Disguise is still a factor in the formation of a dream; its use is invoked at the behest of the ego and its defenses as pressured by the superego so as to avoid the direct expression of anxiety-provoking id wishes and reflections of their genetic (early childhood) roots.

The more recent versions of the structural model afford the ego's capacities for relatedness a major role in emotional life (Langs, 1998a). These interpersonal, intersubjective, and self-psychological theories are not, however, grounded in definitive models of the mind, nor are they established with strong adaptive positions. They tend to stress the role of early and later relationships as they offer empathy and support or the reverse, empathic failures and harm. Relationships and interpersonal transactions are seen as the primary sources of conflict and of aroused pathological id drives, issues that are mediated by the ego and its defenses. Object relations, as they are termed, are thereby considered a major determinant of emotional health and dysfunction (Slavin & Kriegman, 1992).

This shift in emphasis toward interpersonal transactions again is cast in weak adaptive terms and with little regard for deeply unconscious features of therapists' interventions. Conflicts, too, are seen more in terms of conscious than of unconscious issues (Winston & Winston, 1998). As a result, allusions are made to surface struggles and general relationship experiences and their evident meanings, in lieu of considerations of specific relationship interactions and traumas and well-defined unconscious conflicts.

Dreams are explored as reflections of interpersonal needs, conflicts, and support. The revised Freudian concept of the term *unconscious* as a quality of mental contents and processes promotes a rather general and ill-defined search for unconscious, latent dream contents. Extractions from the manifest contents of dreams are cast as reflections of a patient's mode of relatedness. Dreams are said to reflect the success or failure of efforts to deal with the broad behaviors of those individuals who interact with the dreamer. These latent contents also are understood to embody the dreamer's unconscious view of these relationships and of reality in general. The theories argue that reality is without absolute value and is constructed by a dreamer based on his or her past experiences and inner mental needs and propensities (Langs, 1998a). Such constructions also are made conjointly by patient and therapist, and their nature can be extracted from a patient's dreams.

The results of the dreamwork derived from these psychodynamic models are mixed. Dynamic therapists strive to define the unconscious wishes, modes of relatedness, object relations, and defenses reflected in dreams and to undo evident disguises to unmask underlying latent contents. But much of this work is, as noted, surface oriented and quite arbitrary in that there is no accepted, reliable way to define the unconscious realm of experience or assess the accuracy and effects of these interpretations. Most dynamic therapists tend to limit themselves to dealing with manifest dream contents and their proposed implications. Meanings are extracted from the surface of a dream and there are no efforts at adaptation-oriented trigger decoding. The results are inconsistent in that they reflect a given therapist's theoretical biases as supported by blind spots in evaluating the unconscious aspects of patients' responses to the therapist's dream-based interventions.

Let us now propose some meanings of our specimen dream

in Chapter 2 in view of the structural theory of the mind and its extension into object relations.

The central structural conflict in Ms. Wile's dream appears to involve sexual wishes that are seen as mixed with aggression or violence and as inappropriate or forbidden. The key conflict then lies in sexual and aggressive wishes that her superego repudiates. Relationships with men are considered sadomasochistic and traumatizing rather than gratifying. If efforts were being made in her therapy to resolve these conflicts, the dream would indicate that they had not as yet been successful.

On the whole, classical dream theories and dreamwork currently tend to be based on a relatively simple view of the design of the mind in terms of three systems, with a special stress on the ego and relatedness. The dreamwork is concentrated on manifest dream contents and their implications, and there is an evident arbitrariness and surface quality to the interpretations so derived. What we need is a form of dreamwork that is more systematic, verifiable, and definitively focused on unconscious experience and conflict, intrapsychic and interpersonal.

The Jungian Model of the Mind

In splitting off from mainstream psychoanalysis, Jung (1961, 1974; Maidenbaum, 1998) developed a crude model of the mind that he defined in his own terms. The mind was divided into conscious and unconscious realms, each compensating for the other. He saw the unconscious mind as having two basic components: one is personal and is based on an individual's life experiences; the other, which is universal, is known as the collective unconscious. The latter is made up of archetypes— inherited patterns or forms that are adopted by ideas and fantasies, and also are seen in myths and symbols. As a type of unconscious expression and communication, they are genetically determined modes of psychic functioning. Examples are the anima (the feminine side of men) and the animus (the masculine side of women).

Another major feature of the unconscious mind was what he called *complexes*, split-off parts of the personality composed of affect-laden, schema-like structures that are organized around central life needs and issues; complexes drive human emotional behavior. Jung also acknowledged the existence of unconscious perception, but he did not make explicit use of this mechanism in his thinking.

Based on his model of the mind, Jung saw two levels of meaning in dreams: the archetypical and the personal. To access each of these domains, Jung pressed patients for specific associations to dream elements, linked them to the dreamer's life history and current issues, sought to define the complexes reflected in dream images, and encouraged the amplification of the dream by having the dreamer add images to the original dream. Once the personal or object-level meanings of a dream were extracted from the collection of manifest images and interpreted, Jung shifted to the subject level and interpreted the patient's active archetypes and universal symbols.

In a Jungian interpretation of Ms. Wile's dream, the phallic object may represent a male archetype, as well as symbolize heterosexual conflicts in the patient. Ms. Wile may represent an impaired feminine archetype and the man in the dream an assaultive male–father archetype and animus that, on the personal level, are connected to her sexual anxieties and conflicts. The main active complex seems to involve dysphoric sexual anxieties and conflicts, and the sexual activities in the dream could be seen as compensatory to Ms. Wile's impoverished conscious sexuality and sexual life.

Dreams and Psychodynamic Models of the Mind

Summing Up

1. The psychodynamic models of the mind and dream-work have attempted to account for, and use therapeutically, both conscious and unconscious experience as related to emotional dysfunction.
2. The first Freudian model was topographic.
    a. It postulated three systems: UCS, PCS, and CS.
    b. The basic emotional conflict was said to occur between the UCS and CS systems and to involve forbidden, usually incestuous, wishes and needs, mainly of a sexual nature.
    c. Also postulated were repressive censorship barriers that extract disguises as fantasies and wishes move from the UCS to the PCS, and, although less so, as they move from the PCS to the CS.
    d. For this model, the central feature of each mental system and its contents was that of being unconscious or conscious. Thus, the term *unconscious* was a defining concept in this model of the mind.
    e. Whatever its problems, this model was essentially adaptive; it was concerned with inputs into and outputs from the mental apparatus.
3. The second, or structural, model of the mind defined the psychic apparatus in terms of its functions.
    a. The model postulated an executive ego, an instinctual-drive id, and an overseeing, morally oriented superego, each with conscious and unconscious components.
    b. The defining feature of psychoanalysis, the term

unconscious, was reduced to a quality of experience and became a secondary and vague concept.

   c. While the model promoted the study of relatedness, self, identity, and other functions of the ego and psyche, it also fostered a continued neglect of the adaptive aspects of emotional functioning and symptom formation.

4. The Freudian model of the mind has led to dreamwork developed in terms of the three systems of the mind, including intrapsychic conflict, self structures, and sexual and aggressive conflicts. The focus is on manifest dream contents and their evident unconscious implications. Adaptation-oriented trigger decoding is seldom, if ever, used.

5. Although presented in rather unsystematic fashion, the Jungian model does take into account such aspects of emotional life as the existence of a compensatory mental function that balances the manifest dream against its postulated unconscious implications; the role of nonsexual conflicts, such as those related to aggression, self-fulfillment, and future goals; and the emotional impact of innate mental structures defined as archetypes—universal configurations of expression, structure, and psychodynamics.

   a. Archetypes may be seen as innate configurations and structures that speak for inherited mental structures, such as the emotion-processing mind postulated by the communicative approach.

CHAPTER FOUR

Dreams and an Adaptive Model of the Mind

- Establishing adaptation as the central construct of a model of the mind
- The concept of inherited or innate mental structures and functions
- The emotion-processing mind, the mental module responsible for adaptations to emotionally charged events or triggers
- Conscious and deep unconscious systems of the emotion-processing mind and its modes of adaptation
- The essentials of a strong adaptive position, the communicative approach, as applied to the understanding of emotional life and dreamwork

The strong adaptational orientation of the communicative approach (Langs, 1982, 1992a, 1996b; Smith, 1991, 1998) has led to a return to model making and the creation of the most complex psychodynamic model of the emotional mind fashioned to date (Langs, 1986, 1987a,b, 1992c, 1995a, 1997). The model is, in some ways, a return to Freud's (1900) topographic approach in which the terms *conscious* and *unconscious* once again refer first and foremost to systems and operations of the emotional mind. Although each system is defined somewhat differently in the communicative and Freudian models, the adaptive model stresses the processing of information and meaning; as we saw earlier, Freud's first model of the mind had a similar cast.

The central organizing principle of the communicative or

adaptational–interactional model is that the emotional mind is designed primarily to adapt both consciously and unconsciously to specific emotionally charged triggering events and their manifest and latent meanings—implied, symbolized, and encoded. The model defines a psychological entity constituted as a mental module (Donald, 1991; Gazzaniga, 1992; Mithen, 1996; Stein, 1997), a collection of innate and learned adaptive mental functions that have evolved for the purpose of coping with emotionally charged stimuli. This adaptive module is called the *emotion-processing mind* (Langs, 1992c, 1993, 1995a, 1996b).

Clinical observations developed from the communicative vantage point, including those that pertain to dreams and other narratives, have led to the creation of a new paradigm of dynamically oriented psychotherapy (Raney, 1984; see below and Chapter 5). Its two primary features are postulates regarding the primacy and specificity of conscious and deep unconscious adaptations to external or environmental events and the critical role played by unconscious perception in emotional adaptations. These propositions stand in contrast to the prevailing approaches to emotional coping that are organized in terms of intrapsychic and interpersonally evoked internal fantasies, general adaptive issues and concerns, and conscious perception (Langs, 1992c, 1995b).

The communicative approach to human emotional life, psychotherapy, and dreams forms the basis for the critiques of the theories, models, and dreamwork presented in the two previous chapters. The approach also is notable for having attempted to define empirically and recast the nature of the unconscious domain and for having developed an unconscious validating methodology for dreamwork (Langs, 1992a). The result is a picture of the emotional domain that departs radically from prevailing views.

Dreams and an Adaptive Model of the Mind

The adaptation-centered model of the mind calls for the identification of specific evocative triggering events, as well as an understanding of the processing capabilities of the emotion-processing mind; both stimulus and responder must be considered in depth. Emotionally charged events have both conscious and unconscious meanings and impact, and these, in turn, are perceived and processed both consciously and unconsciously. Dreams are created and recalled as part of these adaptive efforts.

Emotionally charged triggering events have both immediate and long-term consequences for those who experience them. The immediate response tends to be affective and also behavioral, with such affects as fear, anger or rage, and anxiety serving to activate rapid, usually self-preservative, automatic behavioral reactions (LeDoux, 1996). The long-term response involves the conscious as well as the deep unconscious mental processing of the ramifications of these events and leads to responsive behaviors with major unconscious motivations and sources (Langs, 1992a, 1998b).

Given that, by and large, patients in psychotherapy tend to be engaged less in immediate affect-driven behaviors and far more in long-term processing activities, much of it on the deep unconscious level of experience and adaptation, it is the latter aspect of emotional life that is the most prominent concern of dreamwork in psychotherapy. The following discussion thus concentrates on the relationship between dreamwork and the extended or ongoing processing of emotional adaptation.

The Adaptation-Oriented, Communicative Model

Their environment, animate and inanimate, presents humans with a huge array of unceasing emotionally charged events. It is the basic function of the emotion-processing mind to adapt to the stable and changing parts of that environment, including the many levels of meaning inherent in emotionally charged incidents as they are selectively perceived and experienced by a given individual. The frequency and intensity of these events have created a state of emotional overload for the processing capabilities of this mental module (see Chapter 6), resulting in a two-system emotion-processing mind that receives stimuli both consciously and deeply unconsciously. Many emotionally charged meanings are perceived by the emotion-processing mind without conscious awareness, thereby sparing the conscious mind an excess of potentially disruptive inputs.

The basic clinical means by which the design of the emotion-processing mind has been determined is an approach to listening and formulating the material from patients described as *trigger decoding* (Langs, 1992a, 1993; see Chapter 9). This method calls, first, for the identification of the main adaptation-evoking triggering events to which a patient is responding. Second, it requires turning to the dreams and other narratives in a patient's free associations in order to define his or her conscious and, especially, unconscious perceptions of these triggers and their selectively experienced meanings.

Architecturally, the emotion-processing mind is, as noted, organized as a two-system mental module (Langs, 1995a). A *conscious system* receives inputs via conscious perception and

Dreams and an Adaptive Model of the Mind

then processes this directly communicated and experienced information and meaning via conscious efforts at coping. The system has a superficial unconscious subsystem in which consciously registered memories are stored and processed. The recovery of memories from this system is subject to a conscious-system repressive barrier or gradient. Such material emerges either manifestly and whole from this memory-storage subsystem or via narratives whose themes are thinly disguised and easily deciphered.

For example, a male patient's experience of his male therapist's lateness to a session is superficially encoded in a story about a male teacher who was late to a meeting with the patient because, as the patient consciously saw it, the teacher was fearful of intimacy with men. This story encodes an easily recognized representation and perception of the therapist's lateness. It also embodies the patient's superficial unconscious interpretation to the therapist that he, too, was late because of unresolved homosexual anxieties—something the patient had consciously suspected based on the therapist's earlier behaviors and comments.

The second system of the emotion-processing mind is called the *deep unconscious system*. It receives inputs via the subliminal or unconscious perception of emotionally charged events and meanings that are too anxiety provoking and potentially disruptive to be experienced directly in awareness. The deep unconscious system is an adaptive processing system with its own values, executive functions, intelligence, needs, conscience, adaptive preferences, and the like. These functions, which may be thought of as ego, id, and superego capabilities, are very different from those ego, id, and superego functions that operate in the conscious system.

To contrast the two systems, the conscious system is wide ranging in its perceptions, extremely defensive in its operations in that denial and repression are utilized to excess, relatively insensitive to frame-related or ground-rule interventions or triggers, and inclined to prefer modified or compromised to secured or ideal frames for therapy, and in outside life. In comparison, the deep unconscious system is almost entirely focused on a single dimension of human experience, that of frame-related events and therapeutic interventions, consistently inclined toward secured frames, and relatively nondefensive in its operations.

The main safeguards of the operations of the conscious system and other cognitive modules of the mind, which are responsible for adaptive choices and actions (Donald, 1991; Mithen, 1996), lie with the use of denial and repressive defenses (Langs 1996b, 1997). These defenses are inherent in the operations of unconscious perception, in that this mode of experiencing implies the nonregistration consciously of reality events and/or aspects of their meanings; that is, the use of obliteration, denial, deception, and deep unconscious repression.

This situation is the result of a pivotal architectural feature of the emotion-processing mind that involves the absence of mental tracts that could enable an individual to become directly aware of unconsciously perceived and processed meanings. Thus, the human mind universally is restricted by evolved and inherited design features to limiting the conscious realization of deep unconscious experience to encoded representations as reflected in narrative tales, such as dreams. In essence, deep unconscious experiences and processes never enter awareness undisguised.

The deep unconscious level of human experience has powerful effects on human emotional life and the psychotherapy experience. Despite this influence, these experiences do not

Dreams and an Adaptive Model of the Mind

spontaneously break through directly into awareness; such breakthroughs come from the superficial rather than the deep unconscious part of the emotion-processing mind. Furthermore, the effects of deep unconscious experience are, by design, displaced from unconsciously perceived, denied, and repressed triggering events and meanings onto other situations and individuals. As a result, humans are inclined toward unconsciously driven behaviors that prompt them, again and again, unwittingly to react consciously to the wrong person for the wrong (conscious) reasons; the "true" reasons reside in the deep unconscious part of the mind.

By and large, it is only by engaging in validated efforts at trigger decoding that the highly critical deep unconscious realm of human emotional experience can be made directly accessible to the conscious mind. Given that the mind is inherently designed to exclude these unconsciously experienced events and meanings from awareness, it is very difficult to use adaptation-oriented trigger decoding effectively. Because it is, in substance, an attempt to override the natural design of the emotion-processing mind, this pursuit requires a somewhat fearless therapist who is able to help patients to carry it out.

As a safeguard for the validity of this model and its decoding process, an unconscious confirmatory methodology has been put into place (Langs, 1982, 1992a). Thus, an intervention by a therapist using this (or any other) approach to dreamwork and therapy is not considered deeply helpful and essentially correct unless it obtains encoded, unconscious validation in the patient's subsequent dreams and narratives. This type of confirmatory response takes the form of displaced themes and images of well-functioning individuals and positive experiences (*interpersonal validation*) and of encoded narratives that significantly extend the insights developed in the

DREAMS AND EMOTIONAL ADAPTATION

interpretation (*cognitive validation*). The same principles apply equally to interpretations, ground rule–related interventions, and all other forms of intervening.

The Adaptive Approach to Dreams

With respect to dreams, this model sees manifest contents as reflections of the operations of the conscious system of the emotion-processing mind. Beyond the surface images of dreams, two types of latent, unconscious contents are postulated: The first belong to the conscious system as well, and they take form as implications of manifest themes of which a patient is unaware. We may term these latent contents the *unconscious implications of manifest themes*. As indicated, an intervention formulated in this manner (e.g., a statement of the seemingly unconscious implications of manifest dream contents) must be confirmed by the patient through encoded, narrative themes before the comment can be taken as valid and genuinely helpful.

The second type of unconscious content is camouflaged, disguised, or encoded in patients' dreams—and in their associations to their dream images. We may term these latent contents the *encoded meanings camouflaged in manifest themes*. This type of unconscious meaning is accessible only through trigger decoding, and it reflects the operations of the deep unconscious system of the emotion-processing mind (see Chapter 9).

Both types of latent contents are adaptive responses to triggering events, but only encoded meanings come from the deep unconscious system of the emotion-processing mind. In essence, manifest dream images have both unconscious implications and unconscious encoded meanings, and both are determined in light of the emotionally charged triggering events that prompted the dream and its themes.

Key Features of the Communicative Approach

The communicative approach has generated the only psycho-dynamic model of the emotional mind that has the following features.

1. It is strongly and fundamentally adaptive in nature.
2. It recognizes evolved, universal features of the design and processing functions of the emotion-processing mind.
3. It postulates a two-system emotional mind whose systems operate separately rather than as part of an integrated whole, and whose realm of experience, frame preferences, values, and defenses are very different.
4. It sees environmental inputs—external, emotionally charged events—as the prime activators of emotional adaptations. Internal events—mental, affective, and physical—are viewed as secondary adaptation-evoking triggers.
5. It stresses unconscious perception as a key feature of the operations of the emotion-processing mind, far more so than is unconscious fantasy, which plays a secondary role in emotional responsiveness.
6. It recognizes the extreme defensiveness of the conscious system (and mind) when it comes to experiencing and responding to emotionally charged events (triggers) and their meanings.
7. It views the unconscious part of the mind in terms of

two very different unconscious subsystems: superficial and deep. Each of these subsystems has processing capabilities.

8. The communicative model recognizes that the deep unconscious system has a powerful and wisely adaptive intelligence that operates entirely without awareness interceding, in that its communicative outputs always are encoded.

9. It stresses a decoding procedure—trigger decoding—that is organized around the denied and repressed meanings of emotionally charged events and their most compelling ramifications.

10. It postulates that, for patients in psychotherapy, the most powerful triggering events for deep unconscious experience are constituted by the interventions of their therapists. Furthermore, among these interventions, those that involve the ground rules and conditions of therapy are by far the most compelling. (Lest this point be misunderstood, I want to stress again that I am alluding to deep unconscious rather than conscious experience and processing.)

11. It utilizes patients' unconscious, encoded responses to interventions to test the validity of all of a therapist's comments and actions (and extended silences).

    a. The communicative approach itself is derived entirely from unconsciously validated interventions that have served as the basis, and clinical tests, of its theory and techniques.

12. Finally (and this is a critical feature that will be explored in Chapters 6 and 10), it offers the only model of the emotional mind that extensively considers death, death-related traumas, and death anxiety as fundamental motivational forces and aspects of the human con-

Dreams and an Adaptive Model of the Mind

dition, emotional life, dreamwork, and psychotherapy (Langs, 1997). The fact that trigger decoding inescapably leads both patients and therapists to death-related memories and conflicts—to issues of human and personal mortality—is a major reason why this model and its dreamwork are resisted by the conscious systems of the emotion-processing minds of most present-day psychotherapists.

A Communicative View of the Vignette

In light of the thesis that therapists' ground-rule interventions are the main activators of patients' encoded themes, let's try to identify a possible trigger for Ms. Wile's dream and consider how the dream could then be decoded.

We can turn for help to the principle that triggers evoke themes, and themes reflect the nature and meanings of triggers. Thus, all we need to suggest in thinking about this effort is a frame-related intervention (in word or deed) made by Mr. Thorpe (the therapist) that could have evoked the unconscious perceptions reflected in the powerful dream theme of forced sexual contact. One such possibility would be that Mr. Thorpe had accidently (or deliberately) brushed against Ms. Wile as she entered his consultation room. Another possibility is that Mr. Thorpe had arbitrarily and unilaterally (forcibly) raised Ms. Wile's fee.

The trigger of physical contact is encoded in the dream in the image of the man touching Ms. Wile's breasts; that of the fee increase is encoded in the allusion to the expensive apartment. The themes would then indicate that this forced increase in fee was experienced deeply unconsciously as seductive and rapacious; unilateral frame-modifying interven-

Dreams and Emotional Adaptation

tions by therapists are always experienced in the deep unconscious system as instinctually charged.

It is well to note that the key idea is that Ms. Wile would be selecting from the universal meanings of these triggering events those that were sexual in nature. This selectivity would be based partly on the nature of the trigger and partly on her own life history—in which, for example, seductiveness by her father played a significant role. Another patient would stress the assaultive qualities of such interventions, and yet another would respond mainly to the invasive aspects.

The basic principle is that patients unconsciously select from the universal meanings of emotionally charged triggering events those meanings that are most relevant to their life histories and current inner mental states and relationships. Perceived experience is based on both the nature of the event and the inner world of the perceiver. Furthermore, external reality is most clearly defined and validated deeply unconsciously (i.e., on the encoded level) rather than consciously; it is not arbitrarily decided upon consciously, individually, or via direct consensus with others. Indeed, by virtue of evolved design, humans tend consciously to distort or falsify the nature of reality events, while deeply unconsciously perceiving such events with remarkable accuracy.

Further Considerations

For a final communicative exercise, one that will provide a sense of the interplay between triggers and themes, try to make up a manifest dream that a male patient might have after his female therapist had changed the time of his session because she had to be out of the office at the agreed-upon hour.

Dreams and an Adaptive Model of the Mind

As a rule, encoded narratives, such as dreams, contain bridging themes that portray, describe, or represent their evocative triggers. Thus, the patient can be expected to dream about time, schedule changes, and/or a change in a rule or framework of some kind.

In addition, dream themes arising from the deep unconscious system will have power because unconscious perception is invoked only when extremely disturbing meanings have had an impact on the emotion-processing mind. Thus, we also should expect that the patient will encode a number of powerful emotionally charged meanings of the trigger. Here, meanings might pertain to extremes of greed (rather than canceling the hour and losing her fee, the therapist has changed the time of the session so she can collect her fee), unreliability, or inconsistency (the therapist failed to keep to the agreed-upon schedule). These are only moderately strong themes. In addition, we are likely to hear themes of seductiveness (insisting on seeing the patient at a time other than originally scheduled), of entrapment (the schedule change forces the patient to be at the session at an unscheduled time), and of danger of annihilation (which typically accompanies entrapment images). These are the kinds of themes that have a great deal of emotional power.

From that perspective, the patient could have dreamed of being held prisoner for ransom by a woman who is a hardened criminal. If your own proposed dream had any or several of the themes outlined above, or themes that capture other meanings of this frame break, then you may conclude that your answer also was correct.

Some Further Perspectives

Bion (1977) suggested that his readers go through a book of his once, and then read it a second time to gain a full sense of his ideas. Working with dreams in an unconsciously validated fashion and modeling the emotion-processing mind involve a similar process.

Trigger decoding dreams yields vital information and meaning whereby sound models and theories of the mind can be created. This certainly was true of Freud, especially with respect to his initial model of the mind (Freud, 1900). And once a model has been fashioned, it should reveal previously unrecognized features of the emotional mind and of emotional life and psychotherapy, and lead to a revised model of the mind and the use of new techniques of dreamwork. These fresh approaches to dreams should, in turn, lead to further revisions in the prevailing model of the mind and the dreamwork it sponsors—and so on, ad infinitum.

There is, then, a circular process involved in doing dreamwork based on a sound model of the emotion-processing mind. This process begins with clinical observations of the results of the dreamwork, moves to the development or revision of the model, and then proceeds with efforts to obtain clinical confirmation or disconfirmation of the dreamwork based on the model, whose results prompt further revisions, which leads to new phases in the practice of dreamwork.

All in all, there is here an exquisite interlacing of models and techniques, and a sequential unfolding that takes psychotherapists to ever-increasing heights of insight and effective dreamwork. Those therapists who fail to work with an iden-

Dreams and an Adaptive Model of the Mind

tified and unconsciously validated model and theory of the mind not only tend to engage in arbitrary dream-related efforts, but also miss out on becoming involved in the interplay between observation–interpretation and model-theory building—an invaluable way for therapists to learn and grow.

Summing Up

1. The emotion-processing mind is the inherited or innate mental module that is responsible for emotionally charged adaptations, that is, for adapting to emotionally charged triggering events.

   a. The universal features of this module are shaped by developmental forces, nurturing and damaging interactions, and coincidental life events, among which traumas play a critical role.

2. By design, the emotion-processing mind has two basic components, a conscious system whose perceptions and adaptive choices can be realized directly within awareness, and a deep unconscious system whose perceptions and adaptive choices can reach awareness only in encoded form through narrative vehicles, such as dreams.

3. The strong adaptive or communicative approach to dreamwork involves the understanding and interpretation of dream material in consideration of the emotionally charged triggering events that have prompted the dream material.

   a. Conscious adaptive efforts are, in general, reflected in the manifest contents of dreams, and in their evident implications.

   b. Deep unconscious adaptive efforts are conveyed in

these same manifest contents, but they are reflected in the encoded, rather than direct or manifest, meanings of the dream images.

c. Decoding the encoded meanings of dreams is carried out with regard to the triggers to which a given dream is a response. This effort is known as *trigger decoding*.

4. A critical distinction exists between the implications, unconscious for the patient, that can be directly extracted from manifest dream images and themes and the decoding of these same themes toward the realization of meanings that are unconscious for the patient in light of their evocative triggers.

a. Extracted unconscious meanings belong to conscious adaptation, whereas trigger-decoded unconscious meanings belong to deep unconscious adaptational efforts.

5. All trigger-decoded dream interpretations must obtain encoded or unconscious validation to be accepted as accurate and helpful.

CHAPTER FIVE

The Structure and Adaptive Functions of Dreams

- Dreams as narrative, two-tiered communications with both manifest and encoded meanings
- Dreams as communicative vehicles, messengers that convey the outcome of the conscious and deep unconscious adaptive processing of emotional events
- Defining the conscious and unconscious meanings of dreams
- The role of triggers or emotionally charged events in shaping and organizing the meanings of dreams
- Comparing the various models of the mind and the dreamwork they engender in light of the adaptation-oriented communicative approach

There is a strong inclination among patients and therapists alike to believe that dreams are an entirely unique form of human communication, a concept that is not entirely false and yet is not completely true. Dreams may be understood as thinking and imaging while asleep, using a largely, although not exclusively, visual mode of thought. And, in most instances, dreams are scenarios of imagined, and more rarely actual, transactions and events; they are a remarkable form of inventiveness and storytelling.

In the waking state, the experience of a dream may be described verbally through language (the ideal means of communicating a dream) or communicated via drawings or mimetic actions. Recording dreams by writing them down places the dream outside of the dreamer and tends to destroy its dynamic, living qualities, thereby reducing much of the healing power of dreams and dreamwork (Langs, 1988, 1994).

A useful working definition of a dream experience as conveyed by patients in psychotherapy is that of a visually dominated sequence of events that are created and observed during sleep and then, when the dreamer is awake, transformed into language that essentially takes a narrative or story form.

Dreams as Narratives

Clinical study from the communicative vantage point amply indicates that dreams are but one class of narratives that convey encoded unconscious meanings. Indeed, in the emotional realm, every type of narrative communication functions to encode the results of the operations of superficial and deep unconscious adaptive processing efforts. Contrary to general belief, while dreams are unique in the form that they take and in other ways that are a consequence of the altered state of consciousness in which they occur, they do not owe their enormous adaptive value primarily to the fact that they occur during sleep. Instead, they are invaluable as compelling forms of expression because they are one of several evolved narrative means through which humans reveal *in disguise* the operations of a remarkably sensitive and highly adaptive deep unconscious mental system—a system that is, in the emotional realm, far more sensitive and resourceful than the conscious mind.

Dreams are encoded messages that have the potential to reveal, when trigger decoded, the incisive unconscious perceptions and understanding of the deep unconscious system

The Structure and Adaptive Functions of Dreams

with its extraordinary ability to grasp the multiple meanings and implications of active emotionally charged communications and reality events. Dreams also have access to deeply repressed memories that exert a continual, although silent, influence on emotional life. Such memories, however, do not appear directly in manifest dreams, but are encoded therein; they, too, can be uncovered only through the trigger-decoding process.

For most individuals, dream thinking and waking thinking take different forms: the former is mainly visual and the latter is primarily verbal or language based. In addition, dream images often are unrealistic and fantastic, and, at times, are manifestly concerned with events that have not been thought about in the waking state. Most nonsleep thoughts are logical and realistic, except when a person deliberately or inadvertently engages in flights of fantasy and other imaginative activities.

Studies using the communicative approach have consistently found that the fundamental adaptive properties of dreams derive from their narrative qualities. This storied form is shared with daydreams, fairy tales, and myths, but also with the narratives of fiction and everyday life—all of these communicative forms have comparable structures and adaptive functions.

What makes the use of narratives, such as dreams, so special to emotional life?

The answer to this question lies with the structure and communicative capabilities of the narrative form. All narratives, including dreams, embody and express two levels or distinct modes of experience, communication, and adaptation. One level is conscious and accessible per se to the awareness of a dreamer, whereas the other is unconscious and excluded from such direct awareness; in the absence of trigger decoding, its contents are available to consciousness solely in encoded form.

In essence, then, dreams may be defined adaptively and psychodynamically as action-oriented images that occur during sleep and that subsequently are translated into words and narrative language. In their narrated form, dreams are two-tiered communicative vehicles that contain manifest contents and their implications, which are, in the main, directly accessible without disguise to the awareness of the dreamer. Simultaneously, these same dream images, which speak directly for themselves on one level, embody disguised or encoded latent contents whose meanings are not plainly stated or accessible as such to the conscious mind of the dreamer of the dream.

It is important to note that dreams are *messengers* and not mental processors. They are reports on recent conscious and, especially, deep unconscious adaptive operations. And most critically, they encode the experiences and processing of events and meanings that have been unconsciously perceived and worked over by the deep unconscious intelligence of the emotion-processing mind.

Both the manifest and encoded meanings of dreams are responses to adaptation-evoking triggering events and their implications. The two levels of responsiveness are, however, typically constituted as responses to different triggering events or different meanings of the same event. This situation arises because the conscious and deep unconscious systems of the emotion-processing mind are sensitive to very different aspects of human emotional experience (see Chapter 4). This means that dreamwork derived from the communicative approach, which addresses the deep unconscious system, will be dramatically different from dreamwork derived from any other

The Structure and Adaptive Functions of Dreams

present-day school of psychotherapy in that these all operate in the realm of the conscious system.

A Clinical Exercise

Harold Carr, a man in his 30s, was in psychotherapy with Jane Reed, a social worker. Ms. Reed's overall office setting included both the office building where her office was located and a shopping mall that was on the same property. A heavyset guard sat at the entrance to the building, answered questions, and kept a general lookout.

A year into his once-weekly therapy for depression and marital difficulties, Mr. Carr began a session with two dreams:

> He dreamed that a huge muscular man was trying to murder him.
>
> He then dreamed that he was at a shopping mall and discovered that he was naked from the waist down. He was having trouble covering himself and was very upset when he looked up and saw that his sister, who lived in another country, was looking at him with embarrassment.

The Nature of Meaning in Dreams

What do these dreams tell us about this dreamer? What can we say about how they may fit into his emotional life and his efforts at adaptation?

The human mind is strongly inclined to assign meaning to emotionally charged communications; the mind abhors an emotional vacuum. Thus, in general, rather than acknowledging uncertainty regarding emotionally charged messages, therapists are inclined to fill in gaps and voids imaginatively, even though they often do so in relatively arbitrary fashion. Nowhere is this trend more clearly seen than in developing interpretations of dreams.

This arbitrary assignment of meaning is supported by the tendency to think of dreams as part of human emotional life in general, as a broadly conceived way of responding to life's emotional challenges. This type of thinking is similar to how scientists once thought of the air around us, which they conceptualized in global fashion as atmosphere, or how they viewed the makeup of cells as composed of ill-defined protoplasm. Although these are correct terms and concepts, they proved to be so general and uncertain that they served ignorance more than they did knowledge. It was only when scientists became more specific and discovered the details of the components of these two broadly conceived entities that it became possible truly to understand their nature and functions. Much the same applies to the shift from the prevailing psychodynamic approaches to the emotional world and dreams to the communicative approach.

On hearing Mr. Carr's dream in isolation, it is almost impossible to tell how it fits into his adaptive life. A dream is an interwoven image of a dreamer and his or her environment, including the recent emotionally charged events that activated the emotion-processing mind of the dreamer and prompted the production of a dream. Thus, no matter how much we know about a dreamer, we can say very little about the meaning of a dream based on only half of the picture. Truly meaningful statements about a dream and its dreamer can be made only when the entire scene is available for scrutiny: the dreamer and his or her environmental triggers, the fundamental unity of emotional life.

It is, of course, possible to say a few general things about

The Structure and Adaptive Functions of Dreams

a dreamer based on an isolated dream. However, these are weak and highly speculative pronouncements that may have some validity, but are just as likely to miss the point or misrepresent the dreamer's mental state and adaptive resources. If this patient had dreamed that he was running very fast, how would we know whether he was a coward fleeing a challenge or a hero rushing to help a woman in distress?

Consider Mr. Carr's first dream. What does it reveal about him and his emotional life? Is he a murderer in fact or fantasy who is projecting his violence onto someone else? Or is he a masochist who wishes to be killed? Or is he guilt ridden and seeking punishment? At most, we could speculate that he is concerned with violence and death, but we would have no idea why this was the case.

In order to say something meaningful about this dream and its dreamer, we would need to know what had triggered the dream image. Suppose, for example, that Mr. Carr had been badly beaten. The dream would then be seen as a traumatic dream that, with little disguise, conveyed the experience of nearly being murdered. The dream also might reflect, however, a thinly disguised wish for revenge (i.e., to murder his attacker). This trigger would suggest that, on this level, the dream is probably not a reflection of interpersonal or intrapsychic difficulties related to aggression, violence, and rage. That is, the manifest dream would be in keeping with an expected, nonpathological reaction to a severely harmful trauma.

But suppose the trigger for Mr. Carr's dream was his being fired from his job. Here, too, the disguised representation of the trigger—being fired portrayed as being killed—is readily decoded. In this case, the question as to whether the dream reflects a nonneurotic, appropriate view of this hurt or a neurotic, excessive one would be difficult to answer. The knowledge that deep unconscious experience is raw, tends to be instinctualized, and is far more intense and powerful than conscious-system experience would argue in favor of a non-neurotic, unconscious perception.

Or suppose that the dream was a reaction to being refused sexual intercourse by his wife—or the opposite, that it followed having had intercourse with her. What then?

The main point is that the contents of a dream can be sensibly assessed only when their activating stimuli or triggers are known. To say that this dream indicates that Mr. Carr has a problem with aggression and violence is unjustified, and to say that something has enraged him begs the question.

We must conclude that dreamers and their dreams can be understood only when their immediate adaptation-evoking triggers are taken into account. This principle applies equally to the manifest dream and its encoded meanings.

The same precepts apply to Mr. Carr's second dream. Is it fair or meaningful to say that he has exhibitionistic conflicts or that he entertains incestuous wishes and fantasies toward his sister, or mother, or whomever? Does his presence at a mall mean that he's greedy or financially needy, or that he likes to shop or to possess worldly goods?

Here, too, we are dealing with arbitrary speculations and empty conjectures. Suppose the dream had been prompted by his having been intruded upon by a female colleague while he was in the company bathroom. Or suppose it had been evoked by his being seen by one of his sisters while he was having dinner with an attractive woman other than his wife. Or imagine that the dream was set off by his learning that he has lung cancer.

Each trigger would give the dream a different constellation of meanings and afford it a distinctive interpretation. This is

The Structure and Adaptive Functions of Dreams

why placing dreams into a specific adaptive framework is the only means by which we can look deeply and meaningfully into the mind and life of a dreamer, interpret his or her deep unconscious experience of the emotional world, and assess the qualities of his or her emotional adaptations—their strengths and weaknesses.

Two Triggers for These Dreams

Having proposed that the images and themes of a dream are evoked by triggering events and, therefore, encode or disguise the nature and meanings of the triggers that have evoked them, it is possible to speculate about conceivable triggers for these two dreams. But even here there is a great deal of uncertainty. There are far too many possible triggers for these two dreams to be confident that even the best-informed guess will be on the mark.

It is the patient's responsibility to identify his or her most active triggering events and to understand the meanings of those events to which he or she is reacting most intensely. Thus, patients not only must report their dreams, but they also need to discover the triggers to which they are adapting and are dreaming about. As we shall see in Chapter 7, this search for triggers is carried out either through direct recall or by using the encoded themes in the patient's dreams and associations as clues.

The search for critical triggers is often a difficult undertaking because many anxiety-provoking, emotionally charged triggers, and a selection of their meanings, are obliterated from awareness and repressed, and so will go unrecognized consciously by the patient. This will preclude trigger decoding the themes made available through a dream and associations

DREAMS AND EMOTIONAL ADAPTATION

to the dream. The so-called linking process—connecting the abstracted encoded themes to their activating triggers (which is the final step in adaptively processing a dream for interpretation)—will not be feasible (see Chapters 9 and 10). As encoded harbingers of powerfully disturbing deep unconscious experiences, dreams often are repressed or left bare without associations. But when these defenses are insufficient, the failure to recall a critical trigger becomes a prime communicative defense; one way or another, deep unconscious meaning is opposed, and usually excluded (Langs, 1993, 1997).

This is the reason why manifest dreams per se reveal very little, if anything, about the architecture and functions of dreams; they are products of overdefended conscious systems. In contrast, once a dream's triggering event has been discovered, and the dynamic conflicts and issues with which a dreamer is dealing have been identified, it becomes possible to appreciate the role that dreams play in emotional communication and adaptations.

Again, the most critical encoded meanings of the dreams of patients in psychotherapy almost always involve deep unconscious adaptive responses to the ground-rule or frame-related interventions of their therapists (Langs, 1998b). In this case, Mr. Carr's two dreams were triggered by a telephone conversation initiated by his wife to Ms. Reed. She had informed her husband about the call on the day prior to the dream, telling him that Ms. Reed had discussed several incidents that had come up in Mr. Carr's sessions, things that she felt Mrs. Carr should know about and understand.

What are the critical frame-related attributes of this triggering event or intervention?

This trigger is a violation by Ms. Reed of the ideal ground rules of psychotherapy that call for the total privacy and confidentiality of the treatment situation. There are two sets of universal meanings to this frame modification: the first set applies to all frame modifications, and the second to all instances of a particular type of infraction (Langs, 1998b).

Knowledge of these universal attributes enables a therapist rapidly to organize the material from his or her patients around active frame-related triggers and to be on the alert for those meanings to which a given patient is most sensitive. In doing so, however, it is essential that the therapist also be open to meanings that he or she has not anticipated, but can be discovered by exploring the encoded themes in a patient's dream. To do psychotherapy effectively, a therapist must operate with a divided mind: rapidly postulating and understanding a great deal about the patient's material even though it creates a distinct bias, and yet completely open to receiving unforeseen meanings and discovering unrecognized triggers that are reflected in, and are being reacted to through, a patient's dream (and other) material.

What are some of the most pertinent universal meanings of a frame break of this kind? That is, what are patients' consensual unconscious perceptions of therapists who modify the ground rules of therapy pertaining to total privacy and confidentiality?

Even though the patient had given permission for his wife to call Ms. Reed, the encoded themes will pertain first and foremost to the *therapist's* need to modify the framework or ground rules of the therapy in this manner. Second, because of the patient's active role in this frame break, the encoded themes will involve unconscious perceptions of his own unconscious needs in this regard (and third, of his wife as well).

There are many universal meanings to these two frame modifications, which often go hand-in-hand. In this case, they would apply to all concerned, especially the patient and the therapist, but here I refer to these meanings in terms of the patient's unconscious perceptions of the therapist.

Therapists' violations of the total privacy and confidentiality of a psychotherapy are seen deeply unconsciously by patients as reflections of the therapist's fears of intimacy with a patient, a view that is based on recognizing the therapist's need to allow a third party into the therapy. Also intrinsic to this action are betrayals of trust; inappropriate exposure to others of the patient, and also the therapist; violence and harm directed against the patient; sexualization and fear of the relationship with the patient; and a sexualized attraction to the outsiders who have been allowed to become third parties to the therapy. This is a sampling of the inherent or universal meanings of this double-frame violation. Each patient unconsciously will select his or her personally colored responses from these ever-present attributes.

What, then, are the encoded themes in this dream? And what do they tell us of Mr. Carr's unconscious perceptions of Ms. Reed in light of her frame-modifying contact with his wife?

The first step in decoding these manifest dreams in view of their trigger is to seek bridging themes—images that connect the dream to the frame-deviant intervention. Recall that Ms. Reed's office is in a complex that includes a shopping mall and that there also is a heavyset guard who sits at the entrance to the office building. Thus, the muscular man in the first dream and the allusion to the mall in the second dream are both bridging images that connect the dream to the therapy situation.

Considering Mr. Carr's need to adapt to this frame-deviant trigger, the dream of an attempt to murder him appears to encode a deep unconscious experience of this frame break as doing violence to him. Frame violations inherently evoke in-

The Structure and Adaptive Functions of Dreams

stinctualized deep unconscious experiences, so the sense that someone is trying to destroy him is not a distortion or an invalid perception. It is, instead, a reflection of the enormous psychological harm that this kind of frame break causes patients.

Notice, too, that the therapist is represented here by the male guard, a multidetermined disguise unconsciously chosen by the patient because, first, it bridges over to the therapist's office and, therefore, to the therapist; second, it expresses an unconscious perception of the aggressive qualities of the contact between Mrs. Carr and Ms. Reed; and third, it embodies the patient's personal historical or genetic link to this frame break in that, as a child, he had been beaten repeatedly by his father.

The second dream encodes the inappropriate exposure of the patient through the revelations made by his therapist to his wife. Here, the wife is represented by Mr. Carr's sister, whom he unconsciously selected because of an incident in his teens when he had exposed himself to her and she had revealed what he had done to their parents—evoking a violent punishment from his father.

The themes in these dreams, then, convey on the encoded level two of Mr. Carr's valid, personally selected unconscious perceptions of Ms. Reed based on the adaptation-evoking, frame-modifying trigger of her talk with his wife. Rather than reflecting fantasy-based projections onto his therapist, the themes indicate how Ms. Reed had traumatized Mr. Carr in ways that repeated, in some form, earlier traumatic incidents with his father. In adapting to emotionally charged triggers, a given patient's unconscious perceptions are shaped, in part, by the ways in which present events somehow repeat past traumas. There is little or no misperception or transference distortion involved in the operations of the deep unconscious system of the emotion-processing mind; in contrast, emotionally charged, conscious system perceptions are often distorted or erroneous.

The Basic Structure of a Dream

This adaptation-oriented study of Mr. Carr's dreams facilitates the identification of the main structural features of dreams.

With regard to the adaptive or coping responses expressed in dream images, we can say that dreams have at least two levels of meaning and reflect two distinct modes of adaptation. The first level is manifest and reflected in the surface of the dream. It is revealed through a direct examination of the dream's contents per se and the extraction of their implications considering the prevailing evocative triggering events. This level of communication is related to the operations and coping strategies of the conscious system of the emotion-processing mind.

The second level of meaning and adaptation is latent and encoded. It is revealed when a dream is trigger decoded, when its disguises are unmasked in light of their evocative triggering events. This level of communication is related to the operations and coping strategies of the deep unconscious system of the emotion-processing mind.

These two mental systems function on the basis of dramatically different adaptive tactics and preferences. They embrace very different constellations of needs, values, defenses, and the like. As a result, dreamwork that pursues the interpretation of a manifest dream takes a therapist to a world of experience and adaptation that is very different from that accessed

The Structure and Adaptive Functions of Dreams

through dreamwork carried out by those who also would interpret a dream's encoded, latent contents.

The choice of approach depends on the model of the mind a therapist uses. Given its evolved defensive predilections, however, the mind is naturally inclined to seek the lesser truths of the manifest dream and to avoid the more powerful truths of encoded dream contents. Thus, the use of trigger decoding provides a way to discover the emotional secrets of nature that the mind avoids consciously, and yet conveys via camouflage—secrets that nevertheless are the deepest source of emotional ills and whose mastery can contribute most effectively to lasting emotional health.

Models of the Mind Revisited

Models of human emotional life and dream formation, such as behaviorism and neuroscience, that bypass the mind avoid the psychological realm entirely, keeping their distance from the dreaded but all-important realm of deep unconscious experience. Models that stress inner mental processes and the generalities of interpersonal transactions without a definitive consideration of specific external triggers, such as those developed by the cognitive, interpersonal, and psychodynamic approaches, explore the implications of manifest dreams, but also steer clear of deep unconscious experience. Only the communicative model calls for trigger decoding and an unswerving commitment to exploring the deep unconscious realm of experience.

In terms of the two dreams reported by Mr. Carr, the behavioral model would seek reflections of the patient's maladaptive actions in these manifest dreams. The dreams would prompt the therapist to ask the patient if he was inclined to retreat from danger, had a problem exposing himself sexually, or behaved badly in interactions with women. The therapeutic effort would unfold according to the answers to these questions, which are, of course, shaped by the therapist's theory of emotional dysfunctions.

The cognitive therapist would ask questions about Mr. Carr's schemata, beliefs, and affects. Does he view men as murderers? Does he believe that exposing himself to women alleviates his sexual anxieties? Does he have a heterosexual schema that is disturbed by incestuous needs?

Psychodynamic and interpersonal therapists would ask such questions as: Does Mr. Carr have unconscious murderous wishes toward men and his father or unconscious masochistic wishes—or both? Is there an incestuous problem with his sister, and how does it affect his relationships with women? What impulses or fantasies is he projecting onto the therapist in the transference—is it a murderous wish of his own, or an incestuous wish to expose himself to her sexually?

And, finally, the communicative therapist would ask: What frame-related intervention by his therapist has evoked Mr. Carr's unconscious perceptions of Ms. Reed? What early traumas has this intervention reenacted? How is the patient trying to cope with the unconsciously experienced effects of the intervention? As can be seen, these are the only questions developed in terms of the precept that specific, emotionally charged, environmental or reality events, usually frame related in nature, evoke specific deep unconscious responses that are then encoded in dreams. Again we see that the compelling secrets of nature lie in its details.

The inferences that a therapist would make regarding Mr. Carr's mental status, psychopathology, and maladaptations—indeed, the entire picture that a therapist would have of this

The Structure and Adaptive Functions of Dreams

patient—are dramatically different depending on the model of the mind and approach to dreams that the therapist uses. Most tellingly, in assessing the meanings of the first dream, only the communicative therapist would stress the violent aspects of the *therapist's* frame break rather than a basic problem with violence that simply resides in, and is being projected by, the *patient*. Whatever Mr. Carr's problems with aggression might be, they have, in this view, been activated by an inherently assaultive frame break by his therapist. As for the second dream, the communicative therapist would locate the primary problem with the *therapist's* rather than the *patient's* exhibitionism. His needs to expose himself are, for the moment, secondary, even though they led him to act out exhibitionistically with his wife and therapist through the frame break he had sanctioned and to stress this quality of what the therapist had done.

The key point is that, with each dream, all of the other models of the mind would lead to an exclusive focus on the patient's emotional pathology, whereas the communicative model would lead first to the therapist's emotional pathology and only then to that of the patient. The differences in these conceptualizations lie with the contrasting models of how the emotion-processing mind operates: the communicative model places unconscious perception first and unconscious fantasy second; the other models place fantasy, or inner mental contents interpersonally evoked, first, and they do not consider unconscious perception at all. There is, then, a world of difference in the dreamwork and interpretations offered by communicative and noncommunicative psychotherapists.

Summing Up

1. Dreams are layered with meaning, manifest and encoded.

2. Dreams function as messages that reflect adaptive responses to emotionally charged, triggering events. They are not simply expressions of the inner mental world of the dreamer, nor do they serve mainly to convey general reactions to ill-defined emotional relationships and issues in the life of the dreamer.

3. Manifest contents per se convey directly dramatized and indicated meanings and speak for a variety of implications of the dream's surface images and their meanings. They also may convey thinly disguised encoded messages. This level of communication and experience is connected with the operations of the conscious system of the emotion-processing mind.

4. The heavily encoded messages in dreams arise from deep unconscious adaptive responses to repressed triggering events or to the repressed meanings of consciously known triggers.

5. By and large, the manifest and encoded meanings of dreams transmit responses to different triggering events and/or to different meanings of known triggers. This arises because the conscious and deep unconscious systems of the emotion-processing mind are sensitive to very different aspects of human emotional experience.

6. Dreams are but one form of the narrative mode of human communication. As all narrative tales possess the essential properties of double-meaning, two-layered communicative expression, it follows that the principles

The Structure and Adaptive Functions of Dreams

and techniques that apply to dreamwork may be used with any story told by a patient in the course of a session.

7. Aspects of these ideas have been formulated in another form by Haskell (1989): dreams and stories are reflections of the analogical mode of thinking and information processing. That is, the human mind uses two modes of thought, one that is direct in its representations (an image is what it says it is) and another that operates via analogy (an image is something other than what it says it is, and that something is comparable to the manifest expression). The former mode is, in my terms, the manifest level of communication and experience, and the latter mode is the deep unconscious or encoded level of communication and experience.

CHAPTER SIX

An Evolutionary History of Dreams

- The importance of an evolutionary (historical or distal) perspective on the emotion-processing mind and emotional life
- The related significance of proximal (personal genetic and immediate environmental) causes of the adaptive responses of this same mental module
- The essentials of a modern-day, revised neo-Darwinian theory of evolution
- A historical, evolutionary scenario pertaining to the emotional environments and mental coping capacities of the hominid species
- The critical role played by the emergence of language
- The role of dream reports in the evolution of the adaptive capabilities of the emotion-processing mind

As indicated earlier, Darwin's theory of evolution and its modern-day neo-Darwinian addenda constitute the fundamental subtheory of biology (Dawkins, 1976; Mayr, 1983; Plotkin, 1994, 1997; Dennett, 1995). In my many years of work as a psychotherapist and psychoanalyst, I have explored numerous supplementary perspectives in order to better understand the emotional mind and therapeutic process—model making, physics, mathematics, archaeology and anthropology, neuroscience, animal studies, psychology, systems theory, and such. In the course of these efforts, I found that the theory of evolution—the investigation of adaptations and their extended histories—offers the most exciting, illuminating, and compelling set of ancillary ideas and insights available from other disciplines. In fact, an understanding of evolutionary science and the evolution of the emotion-processing mind has had far-reaching effects on both the theory and techniques of communicative psychotherapy, including its unique form of dreamwork.

If we take rapid-eye-movement (REM) sleep as a physical criterion of dreaming, we find that all mammals (except the spiny anteater) show some kind of dream-related activity. On the other hand, if we take the psychological criteria that dreams are imaginary, sensory inner mental experiences or visual/narrative modes of thinking that take place during sleep and that are reported in some form while awake, we are dealing with aspects of dreaming and of dream reporting that are uniquely human. This is especially so when dreams are translated into language-based communicative vehicles.

It thus appears that an understanding of the long-term history of dreaming and the recall of dreams requires a grasp of the evolutionary histories of mimetic and language-based communication. Concentrating on the evolution of the mind, with special emphasis on the emotion-processing mind and narrative expression in the context of the evolution of emotional adaptations, I propose an evolutionary scenario or adaptationist program, as it is called (Gould & Lewontin, 1979; Lewontin, 1979; Mayr, 1983; Tooby & Cosmides, 1990). In this scenario, the evolutionary forces or selection pressures that shaped the nature and adaptive functions of dreams are identified and clarified as a means of helping us to understand why dreams are, as currently configured, two-tiered, manifest and encoded, communicative vehicles.

The Theory of Evolution

The basic theory of evolution is that of favored descent through the natural selection of effective adaptive organs in response to ever-changing environmental conditions (Dawkins, 1976; Plotkin, 1994; Dennett, 1995). The theory envisions the existence of mutations, natural variations, genetic drift, and other mechanisms of genetic change within the individuals belonging to a given group of organisms or species. These genetically based variants compete for survival and reproductive success in the environment that prevails for a given epoch. Those variants that are most effective in these pursuits are favorably reproduced through a passive but essential process termed *natural selection*. The successful variants, along with new ones that have arisen through spontaneous mutations, then respond to a freshly configured set of environmental conditions by competing once again for both survival and reproductive success, and so on in never-ending cycles.

There are several different neo-Darwinian theories of evolution, of which the selfish-gene theory of Dawkins and others is the most commonly accepted version (Dawkins, 1976; Slavin & Kriegman, 1992; Plotkin, 1994; Dennett, 1995). The key addenda revolve around the thesis that natural selection is not centered on the survival and favorable reproduction of either the individual or the species, but is genocentric; that is, it is focused on the reproduction of adaptively effective genes and is driven by efforts of organisms to ensure the reproduction of a species' "gene pool." The issue, therefore, is not one of individual fitness to an environment, but of the fitness of a species, so-called collective fitness. This concept was developed to explain altruism, the sacrifice of an individual in the service of the survival of others, which was understood as a way of extending a species' pool of genes (Badcock, 1986; Slavin & Kriegman, 1992).

Because of the many objections to this genocentric theory, its rigid translations from genes to behavior, and its highly questionable extrapolations from animal data to humans, a series of latter-day evolutionary theories have emerged (Rose, 1998). A very salutary representative of this new form of neo-Darwinian theory is called *evolutionary epistemology* (Campbell, 1974; Plotkin, 1994, 1997). This approach to evolution contends that the emergence in humans of language, unique forms of intelligence, reflective awareness, and culture (shared intelligence) has created major influences on the processes of adaptation and evolution that must be considered along with genes in understanding these realms. This revised, holistic, multifactor theory lends itself far better than does the selfish-gene theory to an understanding of the emergent properties of the human mind, and facilitates an appreciation for the determinants of the evolution of the emotion-processing mind and its emotionally pertinent mental activities, such as dreaming and dream formation.

The evolution of the hominid line that culminated in our own species, *Homo sapiens sapiens*, is a drama of mutational change and favored selection that involves the brain substrate on which mental capacities are based. Nevertheless, even though the genetic changes pertain to the brain (the genotype), the expression of these genes involves the mind (the phenotype). Thus, our concern here is the mental capacities that interact adaptively with the emotionally charged aspects of the hominid environment; it is these attributes and their underlying genetic basis that have been subjected to natural selection.

In order to explore those mental faculties that pertain to

dreams, we need a meaningful unit of selection (Lewontin, 1979) whose evolutionary trajectory we can investigate in some detail. In this regard, it has proved most productive to take the emotion-processing mind as the key unit for the study of emotional adaptations and dreams because it is basic to all psychological and emotional adaptations and interactions (Langs, 1996a,b); for the use of *relatedness* as the unit of selection, see Slavin and Kriegman (1992).

Setting the Stage for the Adaptive Use of Dreams

For the sake of brevity, the following discussion will be limited to a comparison of early (*Homo erectus* and *Homo habilis*) and modern (*Homo sapiens sapiens*) human hominids. The human mind is composed of a group of mental modules, a collection of organized faculties that have evolved for carrying out a variety of adaptive functions (Tooby & Cosmides, 1990; Donald, 1991; Gazzaniga, 1992; Langs, 1996b; Mithen, 1996). The early human mind had modules for general intelligence and crude language forms, and for social, technical, and natural history intelligence. To these we may now add the emotion-processing mind, a distinctive intelligence devoted to the emotionally charged aspects of social interactions and physical events.

For the early human species, knowledge of the environment was highly compartmentalized. Thus, each mental module functioned in its own sphere, with little, if any, transfer of information and skills among modules. Technical knowledge, for example, had little effect on social knowledge, and vice versa. As a result, the overall resourcefulness of early humans was greatly limited and evolutionary progress greatly con-

An Evolutionary History of Dreams

stricted; weaponry, for example, once evolved, remained fixed in design for some two million years.

The reason for this stagnation appears to be connected to the evolution of consciousness. As Mithen (1996) in particular has pointed out, there are two aspects to consciousness: The first is the immediate awareness of an event—so-called event perception or direct awareness—through which an incident is experienced and a memory trace is formed unconsciously that is retrievable only when the event is repeated, as when an animal returns to a watering hole in which it had been attacked. As this type of awareness does not create memory traces that can be called forth at will, it limits learning and adaptive change enormously. It is this kind of consciousness that probably prevailed for the first five million years or so of the six million years of human existence.

The second aspect of consciousness involves self-reflection and the capacity to recall at will and mentally rework an experience in order to learn from it, plan ahead, and advance one's adaptive resources. This reflective consciousness, which allows for processing and learning and for the transfer of knowledge from one mental module to another, appears to have become available to humans quite slowly and to have reached its culmination with the acquisition of language (see below).

Some five to six million years ago, the environment that faced the first human hominids was more complex than those that had confronted their ape predecessors. This was especially true of external demands involving child rearing, pair bonding, social pressures, weaponry, hunting and gathering food, and laws and morals. Although these concerns were relatively simple early on, they increased markedly as the millennia passed. By the time that *Homo sapiens sapiens* appeared on the scene some 300,000 years ago, these environmental selection pressures had become exceedingly demanding and unrelenting. There are indications that these emotional stresses intensified at a much faster rate than did the responsive modifications in the design of the emotion-processing mind; the pace of social changes is very rapid, whereas that of evolutionary change is extremely slow (Plotkin, 1994).

There are indications that the social module played an especially significant role in the development of the cognitive mind (Mithen, 1996). Adaptational needs related to mating, long-term relationships, child rearing, food gathering, group safety against predators, and other increasingly complex forms of social responsibilities and interactions created environmental selection pressures that strongly favored the evolutionary enhancement of social skills and related cognitive adaptive resources.

As these pressures were mounting, two emotionally charged adaptational issues appeared on the scene that were so demanding of adaptive resources that they appear to have tested the limits of the conscious adaptive resources of the emotion-processing mind. Both took place about 300,000 to 150,000 years ago with the emergence of *Homo sapiens sapiens*.

First, there were major advances in weaponry to the point where humans were physically endangered by conspecifics (other humans) to an extent not seen before within species. This situation was aggravated by a strong propensity in humans to react to external traumas, hurts, and threats with extremely violent wishes and actions of their own (an untamed, animal heritage of *Homo sapiens sapiens* remains to this day).

These factors led to an intensely focused awareness of the danger of predatory death and the development of strong predatory death anxieties. They also increased the evolution-

An Evolutionary History of Dreams

ary advantages that accrued to tactics of deception, as compared with truthful or faithful communication (Dawkins & Krebs, 1978; Krebs & Dawkins, 1984; Hauser, 1996; see below), a development of some import to dream formations that are constructed as both revelatory (honest) and deceptive communicative vehicles.

The second development was that of language, which brought with it a set of highly advanced cognitive skills, but also led to a definitive awareness of oneself and one's identity as a separate being, and to the remarkable ability to anticipate the future (Bickerton, 1990; Pinker & Bloom, 1990; Corballis, 1991; Lieberman, 1991; Donald, 1991; Pinker, 1994; Langs, 1996b). This development of reflective consciousness had many consequences. Among them, the articulated realization that death is inevitable for oneself and all loved ones (and others) and the emergence of existential death anxiety are especially important. And here, too, deception, especially self-deception through denial, gained credence as an advantageous survival strategy.

The human function of self-scrutiny (self-observation, self-awareness) and its role in emotional learning is still quite rudimentary (Ornstein, 1991; Langs, 1997). The automatic loss of this capability when dealing with emotionally charged events is part of the major defensive alignment of the conscious system of the emotion-processing mind; it is a key factor in both denial and repression. There also is a defensive human tendency to reflect on trivial, consciously recognized issues and insights to the relative exclusion of powerful emotional problems and deep unconscious experience and insights. These defensive needs carry over to, and tend to limit, the range of accepted forms of dreamwork, and they also appear to be a factor in the failure of some patients to recall their dreams.

A Critical Juncture

We have, then, evidence of a historical unfolding of dramatically increasing demands on the emotion-processing mind to adapt effectively to the growing complexities and stresses of emotional life. These were greatly escalated some 10,000 years ago with the domestication of animals, the ability to grow one's food, and the appearance of urban life. The resultant pressing emotional needs and dangers, which eventually included the aforementioned intense forms of death anxiety, were, with respect to the energies and attention of the conscious mind, in competition with survival-based needs and skills. The quests for food, shelter, safety, and companionship—and, with adulthood, the conception of offspring—were easily compromised by excessive emotional concerns.

The emotion-processing mind developed two types of adaptive responses to deal with the emotional traumas and stresses that threatened to overwhelm the mental apparatus and survival-based emotional and cognitive capabilities. The first are affective responses, which tend to be immediate and to mobilize emergency adaptive resources (LeDoux, 1996). These rapid responses to dangerous situations occupy the entire mind for what tend to be relatively brief periods, during which other functions are largely suspended. But as soon as possible after reacting to the evocative trauma, an individual restores his or her equilibrium and returns consciously to the problems of everyday life and to sustaining his or her existence.

The second type of response is far more extended. It involves the conscious and unconscious processing of the ram-

An Evolutionary History of Dreams

ifications of emotionally charged events, and it can continue for hours, days, or years after a significant incident. This extended processing, sometimes with chronic affective coloring, tends to drain resources from the energy pool and cognitive capabilities of the human mind, and so detract from, and even disrupt, efforts to survive. Historically, when these emotional pressures exceeded a certain limit, they began to compromise the mental adaptive capacities across the human species and to threaten its survival.

The evidence suggests that emotion-processing mental modules operated for a long time as a single-system entity of conscious perceptions and capabilities, supplemented by a superficial unconscious storage and processing subsystem. But with the intensification of emotional impingements beyond a safe threshold, the emotion-processing and cognitive minds began to dysfunction. Drastic changes via the passive selection of mutations and other genetic modifications (e.g., crossovers, genetic drift) were needed to deal with this crisis of survival.

Based on the success of various brain-based mental functions (the phenotype), the genetically determined makeup of the human brain substrate of the mind needed to be modified so that the emotion-processing and cognitive mental modules could operate in a way that did not threaten early death because of an all-consuming overconcern with, and investment in, emotional problems. A most telling response appears to have been the evolution of language, a faculty that facilitated communication, learning, and the development of skills that enhanced chances for survival and reproduction—in part, by greatly improving the adaptive capabilities of both the cognitive and emotion-processing minds. It was through language, as well, that verbalized narratives were born, tales that had their roots in mime, a visual form of communication that appears to have been the first vehicle of shared social knowledge (Donald, 1991)—and a factor in the predominantly visual qualities of dreams.

Narratives and language not only became means of sharing knowledge and of enhancing social and personal growth, but also served as vehicles for emotionally charged communication and adaptations. Thus, language both increased the emotional burdens of humans and enhanced their ability to deal with these burdens—although, once more, demand seems to have outrun mental response capabilities. With so much happening, and with the disruptive effects of adaptive stresses increasing at an exponential rate, mental changes had to evolve and be selected for lest *Homo sapiens sapiens* join the millions of species that have become extinct since life first appeared on this earth; about 99 percent of all species have met with this fate.

Language development required the evolution of both the capacity to speak words properly and meaningfully and the ability to hear those words and correctly and rapidly ascertain their meanings; that is, it had to rely on effective sending and receiving capabilities (Lieberman, 1991; Hauser, 1996). Thus, the solution to conscious-system emotional overload required changes in both how humans communicate and how they perceive and experience what is communicated; that is, complementary changes at both the sending and receiving ends.

The problem of emotional preoccupation increased quite rapidly, and about 200,000 years ago, it reached crisis proportions. A rapid solution was urgently needed and natural selection had little time to solve this survival-threatening predicament; on the evolutionary time scale, significant change usually takes millennia to millions of years.

An Evolutionary History of Dreams

A Naturally Selected Solution

What type of mind did natural selection favor as a way to solve this problem of conscious-system overload? The primary answer is twofold: survival (of genes, species, individuals, and groups; Plotkin, 1997) was fostered on the sending side by selecting minds that were capable of unconscious communication, and on the receiving side, by favoring minds that were capable of unconscious perception. Both solutions were highly defensive and involved a reduction in environmental impingements, both receptive and expressive. Thus, these selections entailed considerable cost in the form of denial and knowledge reduction regarding the emotional terrain; obliteration was the expensive but species-saving emergency solution favored by natural selection.

These evolved unconscious capacities spared both the sender and receiver of emotionally charged messages the conscious experience of many anxiety-provoking and potentially disruptive meanings of traumatic communications and events. Minds were favored that could send bilevel or double-meaning messages, with one set manifest and the other encoded—a miracle of defensive communicative engineering that is seldom appreciated for its remarkable ingenuity. Similarly, also favored were humans who had evolved the remarkable ability to perceive and register complex emotionally charged events and their most disturbing unconscious meanings outside of awareness. All told, this appears to be how the realm of deep unconscious experience and intelligence was born.

As for basic design, these developments were based on the emergence of two-system emotion-processing minds—one system operating with a direct connection to awareness, and the other without such a connection available to it. Two-system minds are able greatly to reduce the emotional load on the conscious system of the emotion-processing mind and on the other cognitive modules. They do so by protecting the conscious mind with an extensive use of the defense of denial, supported by the subsequent use of repression and other communicative and psychological defenses (Langs, 1996b, 1997). These mechanisms maintain the deep unconscious status of impingements that are initially prevented from gaining access to awareness; that is, emotionally charged stimuli or triggers that are perceived unconsciously.

From another perspective, these developments may be seen to involve an increase in the conscious and unconscious use of deception, a form of expression with evident survival advantages (Dawkins & Krebs, 1978; Krebs & Dawkins, 1984; Nesse, 1990b; Hauser, 1996). A human's deception of others is far more than a conscious survival tactic that is used when faced with a predatory threat. It is a common feature of conscious communication used in the service of gaining the upper hand in relationships. Deception also is used unconsciously in interactions with others as a means of concealing murderous impulses and inappropriate sexual wishes. It is, as well, a way of concealing knowledge of others, factual and emotional, whose revelation would evoke undue personal anxiety and retaliatory responses.

Thus, deceiving others enhances human survival by concealing or camouflaging inner needs and impulses directed toward those who would respond by endangering the emotional state, and, at times, the life, of the sender of such messages. Both the consciously deliberate and the unconsciously inadvertent use of deception favor modes of communication

An Evolutionary History of Dreams

that either falsify or disguise dangerous truths. The latter is an essential feature of dream expressions.

Self-deception also enhances survival. It is a reaction within oneself to perceptions of others whose awareness would create extremes of anxiety and vengeful or punitive actions that could threaten that survival. It also is directed against the awareness of the inevitability of death and against the harm one has done to others and inappropriate sexual wishes toward others that would evoke inner guilt and acts of self-punishment, and/or inspire violent forms of retaliation by other individuals.

Minds capable of such compromised communicative expressions were favored by natural selection. Given that the emotion-processing mind is an adaptive module designed to deal with environmental events, it appears that denial, communicative deception and obliteration, and the shutting down of reflective awareness should be recognized as the primary means of psychological defense, and repression seen as playing a supporting role. All of these mechanisms serve to bypass the conscious registration and processing of overburdening, emotionally charged stimuli and meanings.

This design solution is, as noted, quite costly to humans and their emotional adaptive pursuits because, in essence, it entails the loss of the most critical meanings of emotionally relevant experiences and puts an individual in a world filled with deceptions of which he or she is mostly unaware. Furthermore, these defenses facilitate the unconscious use of displacement, which places human emotional behaviors under the influence of unconscious motives. The unconscious use of this mechanism prompts many actions that are inappropriate to reality considerations. Indeed, the huge cost of this highly compromised (and, in the long run, probably temporary) evolutionary solution, with its knowledge reduction and deceptive qualities, is an indication of the urgency of the problems caused by emotional overload and the inadequacies of current solutions.

The Evolved Role of Dreams

Where do dreams come into this story? The answer lies with the development of language and the role of narratives in that evolution. Language is best suited for definitive messages, and narratives are the ideal vehicle for double-meaning communication. Pictures, gestures, and feelings or affects are too indefinite with respect to conveyed meaning to allow for the kind of precision of expression required to impart emotionally charged information and meaning. Language also is a very rapid way of communicating (Lieberman, 1991; Hauser, 1996), and it can express in definitive fashion multiple (condensed) perceptions and messages—each a response to a different triggering event or emotional meaning. And finally, narratives are an ideal means of expressing deception, both consciously and unconsciously.

Dreams are the quintessential narrative form. They have historical roots in mime and their dramatic qualities enable them to carry both direct and encoded meanings. They are among the richest forms of human expression, and they facilitate unconscious communicative exchanges that involve a huge array of meanings that never directly enter the conscious mind of either party. Indeed, many dreams are responses to dreams reported by others, much as, more broadly, many narratives are unconscious responses to the narratives and other unconscious messages received from others.

As a two-tiered form of communication, dreams also are

An Evolutionary History of Dreams

able to speak for manifest meanings that appear truthful, yet serve mainly to deceive, with the more cogent truth being expressed in the underlying encoded message. Thus, quite remarkably, dreams are able to convey both truth and falsehood simultaneously, and, in addition, to express the truth in an indirect, disguised manner so that is not directly known or appreciated. Dreams, therefore, serve survival, not only by sparing the conscious mind overcharged emotional impingements, but also by enabling one's mind to deceive both others and oneself in the service of defense and survival.

The Role of Condensation

As is true of all narratives, dream images are products of the mechanism of condensation in at least six different ways:

1. They condense manifest and encoded meanings.
2. They condense conscious and deep unconscious reactions.
3. They condense into a single dream element reactions to several different triggers.
4. They condense different reactions to the same triggering event.
5. They condense several different narrative tales into each single dream element or image.
6. They condense the truth with lies or deceptions.

As a result, dreams operate as narrative tales that express a rich multiplicity of information and meaning—highly accurate yet quite deceptive. This evolved feature of dreams calls for dreamwork that can unravel the many perceptions, meanings, and deceits that are packed into dream images; that is, efforts that can appropriately undo the automatic use of condensation.

Expanding Dream Imagery and Narrative Themes

To this point, these discussions have primarily concerned dreams per se. But in order to reveal the multifaceted richness of dream imagery, patients need to associate to the elements or images of a manifest dream, and to do so by producing fresh narrative tales, or additional vehicles of encoded expression. Indeed, with few exceptions, the associations to a dream are more powerful and revealing than is the manifest dream itself. In principle, dreams are dreamed to be narratively associated to, rather than to be analyzed.

Quite remarkably, the human mind is able to generate manifest dream elements that condense a multiplicity of encoded narratives; there always are several potential storied associations to each element of a dream. And for their part, each of these associated anecdotes encodes a complex and rich series of unconscious perceptions of the ramifications of one or more emotionally charged triggering events (see Chapter 9). This kind of condensation and multiple representation is an attribute of all dreams and, further, of all origination narratives—stories of any kind that are told in the course of a therapy session with the purpose of serving as points of departure for guided associations to each dream element (see Chapter 10 for details).

The complexity of human emotional life thus has been a major selection factor that has led natural selection to favor minds that are capable, first, of receiving many potentially

An Evolutionary History of Dreams

disturbing emotionally charged meanings outside of awareness; second, of processing that information and meaning unconsciously; and third, of communicating the results of these adaptive processes through encoded narrative vehicles, particularly dreams. Simultaneously, natural selection has favored minds that are able to express both emotional truths and emotional deceptions. The latter enhance survival mainly by enabling individuals to avoid interspecies warfare and intensely disruptive feelings of guilt and the need for self-punishment.

Further Considerations

The experience of dreaming and the use of narrative language to convey the nature of dream events and images allow for the expression of themes that involve two-tiered, conscious and unconscious, communication. Dreams came about in response to the overload of emotional stresses with which the evolving human species was confronted daily. They play a special role in human emotional adaptation in that, first, they are messengers loaded with encoded meaning and wisdom; second, they can convey both truth and self-protective deceptions; and third, they are mental and not behavioral responses to emotionally charged triggers. We are virtually paralyzed when dreaming.

Dreams provide a unique opportunity for the discovery of deep unconscious perceptions and meanings, and the unconscious use of deceptions of others and self. These revelations are possible primarily, if not exclusively, through the process of *trigger decoding*—unmasking the encoded meanings of a dream in light of its evocative triggers.

Dreams are a way station in a conscious and unconscious

adaptive sequence that begins with an emotionally charged triggering event and ends with both a communicative and a behavioral response. Whereas we, as therapists, generally begin an effort to understand a patient's emotional difficulties by turning to his or her dreams, we actually should begin with the triggering events and move forward from there; as noted, a dream is at the end rather than at the beginning of an adaptive sequence.

Because the deep unconscious processing efforts that are encoded in a dream network are so remarkably perceptive and wise, a dream is a potentially resourceful response to a triggering event in that it condenses a multitude of solutions to a multitude of evocative, emotionally charged adaptive challenges. Some of these solutions involve consciously known triggers and can lead to directly recognized, consciously appreciated resolutions to mental and interpersonal conflicts that can prompt effective behavioral responses to the triggering events at issue.

But the most compelling adaptive responses reflected in dreams tend to involve denied and repressed triggers, and to be encoded in a dream's manifest contents and the patient's associations to these contents. With this in mind, we can see why it can be said that only the patient can associate to his or her dream, and only the patient knows the meanings of a dream, even though most of that knowledge is encoded and unconscious rather than straightforward and conscious. By and large, a therapist who is capable of trigger decoding dream material is needed to enable a patient to realize consciously the deep unconscious knowledge disguised in a dream.

Natural selection has chosen minds, then, that generate their most constructive adaptive solutions outside of awareness. These resolutions appear in dreams in encoded form,

An Evolutionary History of Dreams

and they are not directly accessible to awareness. As a result, without trigger decoding, these remarkably wise emotional insights are not available for adaptive response, and they do *not* influence the consciously orchestrated adaptive behaviors and choices that take shape as reactions to triggering events. Furthermore, as noted earlier, this arrangement fosters unconsciously motivated displaced reactions to triggers that often entail interpersonal dysfunctions, symptoms, and misdirected actions.

This is a strange state of affairs: the most effective adaptive resource in the emotion-processing mind as currently designed lies within a deep unconscious intelligence whose wisdom is unusable unless the dreamer engages in trigger decoding (see Chapter 9). Yet, at the same time, the effects of deep unconscious processing misdirect the actions and choices made by a dreamer in his or her life.

This is, as noted, a very expensive response to emotional overload. And it is further aggravated by the effects of a second deep unconscious constellation, the fear–guilt subsystem, that, in contrast to the wisdom subsystem, does have direct unconscious effects on conscious adaptations. Much of this seems to have evolved as a way of curtailing human inclinations toward aggression and vengeance, as well as a means of restricting the fears of, and reactions to, existential death anxiety by locating many of its effects outside of direct awareness (Langs, 1997).

The main hope for overcoming these limiting and expensive design features of the emotion-processing mind is in the realization that humans are not enslaved by their genetic makeup, but have individual and shared intelligences that can override genetic forces (Plotkin, 1994, 1997). The use of this intelligence to trigger decode dream imagery is a major expression of this potential. Both patients and therapists are

Dreams and Emotional Adaptation

born encoders, but neither are born decoders. The much-needed ability, and effort, to trigger decode dreams goes against the evolved design of the emotion-processing mind. As therapists, then, we must learn how to work with dreams, and patients' material in general, in ways that go against the defensive dictates of natural selection.

An Illustrative Vignette

Pauline Walker, a married woman in her early 50s, was in therapy for a midlife depression with Helene Falk, a psychologist. In the session prior to the dream we will consider, Mrs. Walker had been complaining about her dentist, Walter Manning. She had discovered that he was overcharging her and that he was using antiquated dental procedures. Dr. Falk had responded to this material by commenting, first, that she knew Dr. Manning because he also was her dentist, and, second, that Mrs. Walker's staying with him would be a harmful, masochistic act.

Mrs. Walker began the following session with a dream:

> She is walking on the street with another woman. They come to an intersection and the woman indicates the direction they should take. Mrs. Walker wants to go in another direction, but the woman insists that they go her way, and they do. They're suddenly confronted by a man with a gun, who tries to take Mrs. Walker's purse from her; she resists him vehemently. The man calls the other woman by name, but the woman tells him to shut up. Seeing that the woman is the man's confederate, Mrs. Walker realizes that she's been set up for the crime. The woman tells the man to kill Mrs. Walker, at which point she awakens, feeling frightened.

An Evolutionary History of Dreams

Let's first identify the two triggers for this dream, one within the therapy and the other outside of it.

The trigger within the therapy is Dr. Falk's intervention, which includes at least two ground-rule violations (see below). The outside trigger involves the actions of Dr. Manning as described in the information Mrs. Walker had unearthed about him. The conscious and deep unconscious meanings of these triggers have created and shaped these dream images and their themes—the trigger within therapy far more so than the trigger outside of it. This concentration on the therapist begins as soon as a patient enters psychotherapy or counseling: the actions of the therapist become the primary determinants of his or her deep unconscious responses. Decoding the most pertinent meanings of this dream in light of its within-therapy triggers will enable us to appreciate the adaptive value of dreams and their evolved role in unconscious communication.

Again, decoding dreams requires that a therapist maintain a divided approach: On the one hand, he or she must sustain an open mind to facilitate the discovery of unanticipated triggers, unexplained themes, unfathomed meanings, and missed triggers. On the other hand, a therapist's mind must be well informed—capable of cautiously using theory, knowledge of the patient, and an understanding of the human psyche and of the ramifications of triggering events in order rapidly, although tentatively, to formulate the meanings of a dream (and associations to the dream) reported by a patient.

Without using one's knowledge of the emotional domain, it is virtually impossible, in a 45- or 50-minute session, to sort out the multiple meanings of a dream considering its triggers. Yet that same knowledge may blind a therapist to the encoded meanings of a narrative message that pertain to a trigger that is different from the one he or she believes to be most cogent for the moment. In working with dreams, a therapist operates between the Scylla of being blinded by his or her knowledge and convictions and the Charybdis of being too uninformed to realize the most powerful meanings of a dream complex within the time constraints of a therapy session.

It is for these reasons that this discussion begins with an appreciation of the general or universal meanings of Dr. Falk's intervention. Technically, it is both a self-revelation and a nonneutral directive—modifications of the ideal framework of a therapy that calls for the relative anonymity of the therapist and the need to refrain from offering directives or personal opinions to the patient (Langs, 1998b). Among the vast range of currently used and accepted interventions, only trigger-decoded interpretations and frame-securing efforts are unconsciously validated by the encoded images emanating from the deep unconscious part of the emotion-processing mind.

The deep unconscious mind keeps an eye out for departures from the ideal frame, even as the conscious mind ignores them. Dreamwork carried out on manifest levels of meaning generally will not deal with ground-rule issues, but that carried out on the encoded level will always be concentrated in this area; attitudes toward and responses to ground rules constitute the most crucial difference between conscious and deep unconscious values and experience.

Dr. Falk's self-revelation has universal properties that include, and so will evoke themes of, exposure, a shift from a professional to a personal relationship with the patient, a seductive gesture, and a communication that is antitherapeutic and thereby destructive to the therapy and the patient. As for her directive to the patient, it, too, is destructive, as well as being an effort to control the patient and deprive her of her

An Evolutionary History of Dreams

rightful autonomy, demeaning of the patient, and a way of pressing her to be passive and submissive to the therapist. Both interventions are based on the patient's manifest communications, and they thus demonstrate the therapist's ignorance and neglect of deep unconscious meaning. As such, they also pressure the patient to restrict her material and understanding to the surface of communications and to ignore and obliterate unconscious meanings. These attributes accrue to all self-revelations and directives.

A second set of meanings of these comments pertains to the specific nature of the interventions. The conscious meanings of Dr. Falk's informing Mrs. Walker that Dr. Manning was her dentist would revolve around their sharing a dentist and the possibility that he also was fleecing Dr. Falk. The deep unconscious meanings, however, involve the therapist's unwittingly linking herself to a doctor who is cheating his patients and using outmoded techniques. Unconsciously, this is tantamount to a confession by Dr. Falk that she, too, possesses both of these attributes. Her advice to Mrs. Walker to flee her dentist unconsciously recommends (encodes) to the patient that she leave the therapy.

These are some of the risks of working with and commenting on surface material, including manifest dreams. The countertransference-based unconscious, encoded messages that a therapist conveys in such efforts almost always are unconsciously harmful to patients and devastatingly self-critical and confessional. This is the case because of the presence of a highly influential deep unconscious fear–guilt subsystem—a reservoir of needs for punishment and fears of ultimate death—that exerts strong effects on the conscious choices, behaviors, and communications of all humans, including psychotherapists.

Finally, notice that the dream decodes easily in light of the

DREAMS AND EMOTIONAL ADAPTATION

trigger that is outside of therapy—the dentist's overcharges are thinly disguised in the man's attempt to rob the patient. The woman who leads the patient into trouble would then be Mrs. Walker's friend, Edna, who had recommended Dr. Manning to her. In contrast, the deep unconscious, more heavily disguised meanings of this dream are much more difficult to see immediately: they are condensed into these images and strongly camouflaged.

How would we trigger decode Mrs. Walker's dream in view of the attributes of Dr. Falk's two frame-deviant interventions: her self-revelation and directive?

While consciously, Mrs. Walker appreciated Dr. Falk's telling her that she also was a patient of Dr. Manning and advising her to leave him, her deep unconscious experience of this intervention was very different. It is only by trigger decoding the themes in her dream in relation to these frame-modifying triggers that we are able to discover how the disguised themes portray Mrs. Walker's personally selected unconscious perceptions of Dr. Falk in light of her interventions and their unconscious implications.

In substance, the patient unconsciously experienced the first intervention—the self-revelation—as a confession that the therapist also was exploiting the patient and using outmoded therapy techniques. The accumulation of therapeutic errors was so great that the patient felt that her life was endangered. Support for this formulation is seen in the bridging dream theme of a man and a woman determined to harm and rob the patient: both the dentist and the therapist are viewed as thieves.

The second intervention, the advice or quasi-directive to leave the dentist, was experienced unconsciously as an insistent but inappropriate effort to misdirect the patient and lead

An Evolutionary History of Dreams

her into danger. The bridging theme here is connected with the woman in the dream who directs the patient toward trouble.

In the deep unconscious mind, frame breaks are universally experienced as predatory of the patient and they evoke strong predatory death anxieties. The main point for us here is that Mrs. Walker's valid perceptions of these predatory features of Dr. Falk's work with her (and there were many background frame violations that contributed to these perceptions) are unbearable to this patient. In terms of her personal life history, they touch on ways in which the patient's mother had violated and traumatized Mrs. Walker; for example, by confessing to the patient that she was having an affair with a neighbor.

All in all, were Mrs. Walker consciously to understand the therapist's encoded confession, she would be so discombobulated that it would render her terrified, anxious, and somewhat dysfunctional. Were she to reveal these perceptions to her therapist, she most likely would suffer conscious or unconscious retaliatory reactions from Dr. Falk and from guilt over her own murderous wishes concerning her errant therapist, which also were encoded in her dream. By opting for self-deception and for deceiving her therapist by dreaming manifest themes that do not allude directly to the therapist and that encode rather than openly reveal the conflicts at hand, the patient is able to survive this relationship and to maintain a measure of emotional equilibrium, however costly.

We see that experiencing these attributes of her therapist's interventions outside of awareness spares Mrs. Walker a great deal of psychic pain. This defense also enables her to contain her own violent and destructive feelings toward her therapist so that they can continue to work together, albeit without insight into the deep unconscious transactions in which they are engaged. Being compelled to adapt to this kind of complex emotionally charged impingement, with its inherent predatory qualities, touches on the selection pressures from everyday life that contributed to the evolution of the present design of the emotion-processing mind.

Overall, these perspectives on the evolutionary history of, and the likely selection pressures on, the emotion-processing mind help to clarify many seemingly inexplicable aspects of psychotherapy, including the limited or errant manner in which dreamwork is currently conducted by most psychotherapists. This understanding calls for a closer look at the basic precepts that pertain to working with dreams in psychotherapy and counseling.

Summing Up

1. The revised neo-Darwinian theory of evolution is focused on the interplay among genes, environmental conditions, developmental factors, individual and collective (cultural) human intelligence, self-awareness, the ability to anticipate the future and plan ahead, and coincidental life events as they actively affect the process of natural selection.

2. Initially, the main selection pressures for the evolution of the emotion-processing mind involved enormous increases in social contact and responsibilities, and the development of tools and technologies.

3. Language acquisition is the most critical later-day selection pressure (cause of basic design changes), as well as the most important evolved aspect of the resources of the emotion-processing mind.

    a. This resource played a major role in the development of such features of the human mind as self-

An Evolutionary History of Dreams

awareness and self-reflection, the ability to explore and think out adaptive problems and find their solutions in the absence of the causative situation, the capacity to anticipate the future, and, most critically, the awareness of the inevitability of death for oneself, one's loved ones, and other living creatures.

4. It is proposed that, as a result of the development of these uniquely human capacities and their effects on social and other environmental pressures, over time, the human mind entered a state of overload and experienced major threats against survival.

   a. Emotionally charged stimuli became a disruptive set of inputs into the mind and interfered with responses to survival-based needs.

   b. In response to these dangers to survival, natural selection opted for minds capable of unconscious communication and perception, a means of filtering out many of the emotionally pertinent meanings of events so that individuals could effectively deal with the basic needs for food, safety, shelter, and companionship.

   c. The choice of these uniquely human, perceptive abilities was part of nature's strong tendency to select for avoidance and defense, essentially for knowledge reduction, in adapting to traumatic and anxiety-provoking environmental inputs or triggers.

   d. In consequence, many of the critical and affecting aspects of emotional life have been relegated to a deep unconscious, adaptive processing system that operates without direct access to, or strong influence on, awareness and direct efforts at coping.

109

5. The ability to create narratives, such as dreams, was selected in part as a means of conveying in encoded form the perceptions and adaptive operations of the deep unconscious system.

   a. As such, dreams are vehicles that carry to the conscious mind invaluable encoded messages from the deep unconscious system, its experiences of the environment and adaptive responsiveness to environmental inputs.

   b. Deep unconscious experience and adaptive processing are extremely sensitive to significant emotional events and are embodied in a highly effective intelligence.

   c. Unlike conscious experience, which surveys multiple dimensions of the external world, deep unconscious experience is almost entirely concentrated on transactions and triggers pertaining to rules, settings, boundaries, and frames. Unbeknown to the conscious mind, these triggering events exert the most powerful unconscious effects on patients' emotional lives and the vicissitudes of their maladaptations and psychotherapies.

   d. Because the most compelling meanings of dreams are encoded, trigger decoding their images and themes is the only way to enable patients to gain access to their deep unconscious experiences and resources.

6. In sum, dreams in humans have evolved to serve an essential communicative function through which they convey encoded meanings from the deep unconscious to the conscious mind, ready for trigger decoding.

   a. Dreams thus are part of a naturally selected compromise in which many of the anxiety-provoking

An Evolutionary History of Dreams

meanings of traumatic events, including their frame qualities and the ways in which they touch on death-related issues, are both concealed and revealed in disguise.

PART TWO

Dreamwork

CHAPTER SEVEN

The Triggers for Dreams

- Triggers as the emotionally charged environmental events, often traumatic in nature, that prompt adaptive responses in humans
- Classifying triggers
- Ground-rule and frame-related triggers as the most powerful classes of triggering events with regard to deep unconscious experience

Where should we begin our study of dreamwork? As we have seen, there are two inescapable sides to the single entity we are exploring: that of the dreamer and the dream, and that of the environment or trigger that evoked the dream—the individual and his or her adaptive issues.

Therapists who take dreams as their central concern are inclined to turn directly to the dream as their point of departure. They begin with the surface of the dream and, when so inclined, move toward its depths. The risk in this approach is that triggers will be missed or ignored. As a result, the fundamental adaptive functions of dreams will either be overlooked or be treated in a simplistic or erroneous fashion because the adaptation-evoking events that give dreams their shape, meaning, and importance in emotional life are unrecognized.

In contrast, therapists who take the environment and triggers as their point of departure will first define the key adaptation-evoking stimuli for a dream, and then move on to the dreamer, keeping his or her adaptive tasks clearly in mind. They will, therefore, always deal with both parts of the dream experience: the triggers and the dreamers. On that basis, they, too, can move from the surface to the depths, but will do so in a way that is likely to yield considerably more insight than otherwise.

To make this point in a historical context: If, in 1900, Freud had published *The Interpretation of a Days Residues (Triggers)* instead of *The Interpretation of Dreams*, psychotherapists' approaches to both dreams and emotional life would be far different from what they are today—far more organized around issues of adaptation than is now the case.

The Definition of Triggers

Triggers are the emotionally charged environmental events that activate the emotion-processing mind and lead to the production of dreams and their narrated recall. The most powerful triggers are external to the dreamer. In humans, there also are important self-action triggers, especially those that are destructive to others and frame modifying, as well as internal physical experiences, such as those involving a serious illness. There is, as well, a less compelling group of triggering thoughts, feelings, fantasies, memories, and less serious bodily experiences that also evoke internal conscious and unconscious adaptive responses.

The most active environmental triggers for dreams are always contemporaneous. They are emotionally charged hap-

The Triggers for Dreams

penings from the dream day or emotionally powerful recent events that have not been mastered. In psychotherapy, patients often unconsciously process strong, unresolved, frame-deviant triggers for weeks and months after the event. When a traumatic trigger or a critical meaning of a trigger has been unconsciously perceived and then deeply repressed, it may remain so for the duration of a therapy. Encoded derivatives (themes) will be in evidence intermittently even though the trigger itself is never manifestly identified. In the course of working with such frame-related traumas, it is imperative technically that the therapist *not* attempt to undo the patient's denial/repressive psychological defenses and communicative barriers by unilaterally introducing the trigger. An intervention of this kind destroys the therapeutic potential of processing the trigger and the dreams that pertain to it.

Patients may, for instance, continue to encode responses to unrecognized and uncorrected ground-rule modifications for months after they occur, especially if they involve violations of a therapist's relative anonymity. A not uncommon example of this type of situation is seen when a third party reveals grim news about a therapist and his or her family, such as incidents of serious illness, misbehavior, injury, or death. Beyond these powerful events, most of the compelling triggers for the encoded meanings contained in dreams involve very recent interventions by the therapist, and they can, as a rule, be recovered by patients with some therapeutic effort. Thus, in most therapy sessions, patients are processing active therapy-related triggers that occurred in the previous session or two.

In most cases, there are, in addition, therapy-related background triggers composed of emotionally charged interventions—most often frame deviant, although at times frame securing—that took place in the more distant past. These triggers will remain latent and unencoded until they are reactivated by a contemporary triggering event of like kind. Current frame breaks, for example, call forth earlier frame breaks; current frame-securing interventions call up past frame-securing interventions. A dream is not, however, fully understood unless its most recent triggers are identified and validly subjected to interpretation, after which the reactivated past triggers can be reinterpreted with the patient's current material in mind.

Human beings, patients and therapists alike, are designed mentally to concentrate their coping efforts on immediate threats, stresses, and emotional issues. Clinical study also has indicated that the emotion-processing mind is primarily a defensively oriented organ system that, along with the immune system, has evolved mainly to deal with traumatic emotionally charged triggering events (Langs, 1996a, 1997). While the processing of these events may contribute unconsciously to human resourcefulness and creativity by invoking inventive responses to traumas, the systems of the emotion-processing mind have evolved, first and foremost, to deal with gross predatory threats.

These traumas arise mainly from natural disasters and from the hurtful actions of other humans who pose both great physical and psychological dangers. In contrast to this type of massive stress and danger, the immune system deals with microscopic physical predators, mainly bacteria, fungi, and viruses (Clark, 1995). The emotion-processing mind and the immune system thus constitute the front-line human defense systems against outside assault; the protective functions of the mental apparatus are amply evidenced in dream material when it is adaptively processed.

It is, then, specific, external, traumatic events and the threat of eventual personal death (a potential mixture of external and internal dangers) that are most critical for an individual's emotionally oriented adaptive efforts. Dreams are but one of sev-

The Triggers for Dreams

eral tools that have evolved in humans to assist them in adapting to these emotional threats. And dreams are, as noted, a rich but compromised communicative resource: they conceal, encode, and deceive far more than they reveal directly. Without trigger decoding, dreams contribute little to the unconscious insights needed for sound adaptive responses.

Given the realization that triggers are the critical issue for all humans, including psychotherapy patients, let's turn to the task of identifying the most compelling triggering events in human emotional life and in psychotherapy. They are, as well, the most critical triggers for dreams and their manifest and encoded meanings.

Classifications of Triggers

For patients in psychotherapy, there are two pertinent classifications of triggering events. The first classification divides triggers into those emotionally charged events that have taken place outside of versus within (in connection with) a patient's psychotherapy. The second pertains to the nature of the trigger—the particular adaptive issue with which a dreamer and his or her dream are dealing. This latter group pertains to the classes of events that most strongly activate the emotion-processing mind and prompt the creation of dreams. Essentially, it alludes to what can happen to stimulate significant emotional adaptive and processing activities.

Both classifications are organized differently for the conscious and deep unconscious systems of the emotion-processing mind. Furthermore, the dissimilarities in the triggers to which each system is sensitive are reflected in the differences between the manifest and encoded meanings of dream complexes.

119

When it comes to the locale of the events that have triggered a dream, what is the characteristic focus of a dream's manifest and encoded meanings?

The central areas dealt with by the two levels of meaning in dreams can be characterized as follows:

1. *Manifest contents* tend to pertain to events outside of therapy, and to minimize or convey rather obvious commentaries on those incidents that arise within treatment, including the implications of a therapist's interventions. This reflects the basic adaptive focus of the conscious system of the emotion-processing mind, which is concentrated on consciously known triggers and the rather evident implications of these triggers.
2. *Encoded contents* are focused almost entirely on events within therapy. During the time that patients are in psychotherapy, their deep unconscious systems characteristically are focused on the interventions of their therapists, especially those that are frame related.

Thus, there are striking differences in the adaptive concerns of, and the triggers that affect, the two systems of the emotion-processing mind—conscious and unconscious.

The second classification of triggering events involves the kinds of adaptive issues with which manifest and encoded meanings are concerned. This classification also has different listings for the conscious and deep unconscious systems of the mind—and, therefore, for the manifest and encoded meanings of dreams.

The following are the most compelling classes of emotionally charged triggering events of concern to patients in psychotherapy (for a comparable list for people in everyday life, see Langs, 1994).

The Triggers for Dreams

1. **Manifest contents**: Manifest dreams are concerned with a wide variety of emotional issues—everything from threats to survival to conflicts with loved ones to issues concerning hated or feared enemies. This wide range of concerns is a reflection of the variety of adaptive tasks facing the conscious system, which is our basic survival system and, with the aid of other cognitive modules, is responsible for finding food, shelter, companionship, safety, and resolutions to consciously recognized emotional problems.

The conscious system and its manifest dream themes are also well characterized by what they avoid. Emotional life and its stimuli are layered: there are triggers that have profound effects and those that have much less influence. Manifest contents tend to concentrate on the less compelling issues of emotional life and to bypass much of its power.

It is, of course, possible for a therapist to be helpful on this level of human experience and dreamwork. Resolvable conflicts of some importance exist in this realm. There are, as well, some patients who cannot tolerate dealing with the more serious emotional issues that arise from therapy-related triggers of the kind that are relegated to unconscious perception and processing. For example, the defensive aspects of conscious system functioning and manifest content dreamwork suit some highly traumatized patients who take what they can from manifest-content therapies, much of it in the form of new defenses against issues that are experienced deeply unconsciously. In some cases, this work is sufficient to alleviate aspects of their emotional difficulties.

In general, manifest dream meanings do not deal with those areas of emotional concern that are encoded in dreams.

2. **Encoded contents**: Concerning the triggers for the latent, encoded meanings of dreams, the following discussion

may be seen as alluding to what is avoided by design on the manifest-dream conscious-system level and what is dealt with on the encoded-dream deep-unconscious level.

The encoded meanings of dreams organize around three major aspects of emotional life: ground rules and frames, psychological predatory threats, and the inevitability of personal death. Less often, they also may reflect an assessment of the level at which a therapist is listening, formulating, and intervening (manifest or encoded) and the validity of the interventions being offered by the therapist.

Ground rules, boundaries, settings, and frames create the contextual meanings of events and communications that take place within their confines. They involve the regulations and laws that bestow basic order and structure on human life, which, in turn, offer individuals both safety and opportunities for creative chaos and growth.

The conscious mind has a relatively lax attitude toward rules, boundaries, and frames. As a result, different forms of psychotherapy either make use of, or do not invoke, a great variety of ground rules and boundaries, some stated and others implied. Regardless of their nature, these rules, invoked or omitted, tend to be accepted by the conscious minds of most patients and their manifest dreams portray little concern with their effects. On this level, there are individual preferences, but no universally validated framework for psychotherapy.

In contrast, the deep unconscious mind universally seeks and accepts but a single set of unconsciously validated ground rules for psychotherapy—a position that is alien to conscious needs and thinking (Langs, 1992a, 1998b). In the main, these ground rules include a set place, time, length of sessions, and

The Triggers for Dreams

fee (the so-called fixed frame); the patient's use of free association; the total privacy and confidentiality of the therapy, with no third parties of any kind; the relative anonymity of the therapist (no deliberate self-revelations, opinions, directives, or the like); the use of neutral interventions (i.e., only those that obtain encoded validation); and various implied rules, such as the absence of physical contact between patient and therapist.

Encoded themes will validate a therapist's adherence to these ground rules with positive images of knowledgeable and helpful people and themes that reveal the unconscious meanings of a given secured-frame intervention (frame modifications are never validated deeply unconsciously). The therapist who offers this type of nondeviant frame to his or her patients is experienced as safe and reliable, and as soundly holding the patient, inherently caring and supportive, and emotionally stable and healthy.

The secured or enclosed frame also is unconsciously experienced as constricting and entrapping, and it arouses terrifying forms of unconsciously experienced existential death anxiety (see below). Like life itself, which adheres to the existential rule that it is followed by death, the secured frame offers a lifelike gift, while evoking deathlike anxieties. It is this mixture of attributes that is encoded in dreams in response to secured-frame therapies and interventions, and to secured-frame moments in otherwise basically deviant treatment situations—those in which one or more of the deeply unconsciously validated, ideal ground rules is compromised in the established therapeutic contract.

Encoded themes will support secured frames, but will not support frame modifications, even as such departures from the ideal ground rules find manifest, conscious system acceptance.

DREAMS AND EMOTIONAL ADAPTATION

Modified frames are harmful to patients (and their therapists), but serve defensively as a means of denying the inevitability of death and the unconscious experience of hurtful therapeutic interventions. They offer patients forms of manic defense and denial, but also are unsafe, hold the patient poorly, and are inappropriately seductive and assaultive. Nevertheless, manifest dream contents often will support deviant frames because the conscious system is so strongly committed to defense and denial. This is not the case with the deep unconscious system, which consistently encodes for secured frames and understands the harm done by departures from the ideal framework of therapy.

In terms of events in both everyday life and psychotherapy, the deep unconscious system and encoded dream contents are focused on what is termed *the damage (predatory) group of happenings*. This includes illness, harm from others, loss through death, hurtful accidents, psychological assaults, frustrations, and nonsupport. Physical harm; major psychological traumas, including the experience of frame violations; and death are among the greatest concerns of the deep unconscious system. While the conscious system also deals with physical traumas, it tends to experience a very limited range of the emotionally charged meanings of such death-related events, whereas the deep unconscious system perceives a great variety of quite disturbing implications of these same incidents.

As soon as a child acquires language, his or her identity solidifies, as do the identities of those around the child. He or she also begins to have the ability to anticipate the future. These new skills bring with them the realization that personal death is inevitable, as is the death of others. Thus begins life-long, never-absent, conscious attempts, and, more intensely, deeply unconscious efforts, to adapt to the inevitability of

The Triggers for Dreams

death and the existential death anxieties that this realization evokes.

The conscious system tends to deny death in both thought and action, including denial through the violation of ground rules. Such actions create the unconscious illusion or delusion that the frame breaker is an exception to all rules, including the existential rule that death follows life. It is left to the deep unconscious system to recognize the inevitability of death and to encode sound adaptive strategies pertaining to how best to cope with these issues at the least possible cost. Achieving this goal is all but impossible for the conscious mind because, to date, it has found only one means of dealing with existential death anxiety: costly forms of denial in its many guises (Langs, 1997, 1998b).

We may sum matters up this way: Manifest contents are a reflection of conscious system operations and they tend to deal with the less important issues in emotional life. They are an unreliable source of information and meaning, and serve deception and defense far more than they do truth and openness.

Encoded contents, in contrast, are reflections of deep unconscious system operations and they deal with the most powerful and affecting issues in the emotional realm. They almost always express truth and openness, and will not reflect deception unless the system is processing an extreme trauma (Langs, 1998b).

Thus, although a manifest dream may be tepid or strong, essentially true or false, its contents are available to awareness and can be managed by the conscious mind—however defensively and poorly this is done. In contrast, encoded dreams almost always involve powerful and truthful themes, but because of the design of the emotion-processing mind, they must, as a rule, be interpreted by a therapist. This is, on the

DREAMS AND EMOTIONAL ADAPTATION

whole, the main means of enabling a patient to become aware consciously of his or her deep unconscious experience in order to work through the consequences of the activated, repressed, emotionally charged aspects of a triggering event.

A Clinical Excerpt

William Daniels, in his late 20s, was in counseling with Stanley Barton because he had problems relating to women. A little over a year into the therapy, Mr. Barton announced that he was increasing his fee for all of his patients by $10 per session (from $75 to $85). Mr. Daniels responded with conscious appreciation that the cost of living had gone up considerably and indicated that even though it was an added burden, he could accept the fee increase.

The patient began the following session with a dream:

> He is in a dark hallway with a blonde woman. He's feeling aroused
> sexually and kisses the woman, but she pushes him away and runs off.

In isolation and without a strong adaptive perspective, the best we can do with the manifest contents of this dream is speculate in a general and relatively uninformed manner that Mr. Daniels feels rejected by women—a generalization made on the basis of the main dream image and theme. If we were psychoanalytically inclined, we might also speculate that there is an underlying incestuous issue here. Or we might guess that the patient is using denial, that he is inclined to reject women and is projecting his own needs onto them. The sense that Mr. Daniels is in conflict about his relationships with women seems clear, but that was his chief reason for seeking coun-

The Triggers for Dreams

seling. It is, therefore, a statement derived from a manifest dream that reflects what is already known.

Beyond these speculations, we can move away from postulating inner fantasies, needs, and defenses to suggesting possible triggers—evocative, emotionally charged, reality-triggering events—for this manifest dream. In this regard, we could propose the possibility that outside of the therapy, in his everyday life, Mr. Daniels recently had been rejected by a woman. But this, too, is likely to be either something that he already knows consciously or something he would readily recognize if it were interpreted to him.

In all, these are the kinds of conjectures we might make regarding this manifest dream and its triggers as they pertain to conceivable events outside of the counseling situation. These proposals tend to involve evident triggers and easily seen, superficial, conscious system perspectives.

In moving toward trigger decoding the images of this dream, it also seems to be quite difficult to formulate Mr. Daniels' encoded deep unconscious experience of the frame-modifying fee increase from these manifest images alone (i.e., without his guided associations). There is no bridging theme that connects the dream to this trigger. That is, there is no allusion to money or finances, or to the most evident universal meanings of this ground-rule change, such as exploitation, greed, and aggressive manipulation.

At best, then, we could speculate that the fee increase was experienced deeply unconsciously as a seduction, and that while the patient accepted it consciously, he rejected it unconsciously. Even so, we must acknowledge that we are on shaky grounds here in that we need to have some more material, especially Mr. Daniels' associations to the dream, before we can say anything more definitive. As noted earlier, dreams are dreamed not so much to be interpreted as such, but to serve as a source of associations to their elements and images.

To return to the session, Mr. Daniels went on to say that the dream immediately brought to mind an incident with a woman, Anne Caldwell, whom he had dated three or four times. He had gone to dinner with her on the night of the dream, which was the day after his last counseling session, and afterwards they had gone back to her apartment. He said that he had tried to kiss her, but she had put him off and confessed that she was involved with someone else and felt that it wasn't fair to continue to see Mr. Daniels.

The patient went on to ruminate about how the dream showed how rejected he felt and to wonder how and why he managed to be attracted to women who were unavailable to him. When Mr. Barton asked for some more associations to the dream, Mr. Daniels said that Ms. Caldwell was a brunette, like his older sister. He wondered if he had some unresolved incestuous problem with his sister and recalled that when he was in his early teens, she had seduced him into some sex play, although they did not have intercourse. He then ruminated as to whether the women he dated represented his sister in his unconscious and whether this explained his need to reject women because of their incestuous meanings for him.

It appears that Mr. Daniels' manifest dream is a working over, with little disguise, of the rejection by Ms. Caldwell. This trigger is, of course, outside of the therapy, and his conscious thoughts are focused on this realm. There is, in this respect, the added feature of the self-interpretations by the patient that are directly derived from the manifest dream and his initial associations to its images. This type of intellectualized pseudo-understanding is typical of the conscious system and is essen-

The Triggers for Dreams

tially a form of self-deception—a pretense at insight rather than true understanding. Such efforts often involve turning to a minimally disguised dream image that readily connects to a known conflict and allows for facile pseudo-interpretations. The resultant intellectualized pseudo-insights do not reach into the far more powerful realm of deep unconscious experience and seldom enable patients truly to resolve their interpersonal and intrapsychic conflicts.

This is a prototypical situation in which a triggering event outside of therapy has been a factor in evoking the manifest dream themes and some self-evident associations to the dream. This is *not* the realm of deep unconscious experience, which, in this case, is being obscured from view by the patient's concentration on surface issues. Here, manifest themes are being used to falsify the nature of the essential, active emotional truths of the moment—truths that are encoded somewhere in this dream and in as-yet-unheard associations to its images or elements.

To move toward Mr. Daniels' deep unconscious experience, consider the frame allusions in the stories to this point. They are, first, Ms. Caldwell's dating two men at the same time, which, for a single woman, is a marginal frame violation because she seems to be committed to the other man; and second, the incestuous play with the sister, which is a clear frame break—a violation of the incest barrier, the ground rule against incest.

These frame-related themes pertain directly to the patient's emotional difficulties, but the connections the patient has made to his unconscious conflicts are too glib and emotionally detached to be truly or deeply meaningful. Clinical experience has shown that this kind of concentration on outside triggers and manifest themes is characteristic of patients in sessions that follow a frame modification imposed by their therapists, in this case, the fee increase. This focus on external events is consciously defensive and expresses the psychological use of conscious system denial and repression.

The situation became clearer when Mr. Barton did not pick up on his patient's efforts at self-interpretation and, instead, asked Mr. Daniels to associate further to his dream. After a pause, the patient said that the dark hallway brought to mind an incident from his adolescence. He had been visiting a friend one night, and when he left the friend's apartment, he was suddenly accosted by a man in the hallway, who robbed and badly beat him. He was hospitalized for a week because of bleeding from his kidneys, and there was some concern that he might die.

It is typical to find, as is the case here, that the associations to manifest dream elements are more powerful than the manifest dream itself. Associations to dreams are needed in order to access and develop their most compelling encoded themes and meanings. Notice, however, that the manifest meanings in the associations to a dream belong to the manifest dream complex. They are best seen as extensions of the surface of the dream. Interpreting their meanings directly does not involve trigger decoding, but simply makes use of evident emerged meanings that reflect conscious system activities. In the present case, the new associations pertain to being a victim, to being robbed, beaten, and nearly dying. These themes are only marginally related to the rejection by Ms. Caldwell in that they may well speak of feeling cheated and harmed by her.

With regard to the frame-related trigger within the therapy, we should identify the bridging theme that links the dream images to the triggering event and the power (powerful) themes in the dream network. This will enable us to specify

The Triggers for Dreams

Mr. Daniels' deep unconscious perceptions of his therapist's frame-modifying intervention.

First, the bridging theme here is the allusion to being *robbed of money*. The narrative's power themes—robbery, assault, injury, and possible death—decode as an unconscious experience of the fee increase as a sudden attack and robbery that, in some sense, threatened Mr. Daniels' life. The patient's earlier associations also can be connected to this trigger; they indicate a deep unconscious sense that in arbitrarily increasing his fee, the therapist also was being seductive in an incestuous way, as well as rejecting of the patient and trying to provoke him into leaving therapy.

The fee increase was accepted consciously by the patient as both necessary and harmless, a reflection of conscious system denial, deception, and defense. The subject was then avoided consciously in the session that followed. The manifest dream and initial associations—the allusions to being rejected by Ms. Caldwell and the incestuous sex play with his sister—had been used in part to avoid and deny the more powerful meanings of the frame-modifying fee increase, an intervention whose more terrible and compelling meanings had been perceived and processed outside of awareness. Had Mr. Barton not actively pursued additional associations to Mr. Daniels' dream, the patient's communicative resistances would have prevented meaningful encoded themes from emerging in the hour.

Notice, too, that the encoded themes have validity and are not transference-based distortions based on early-life experiences. Instead, they indicate that the frame-breaking trigger was experienced in some sense as a repetition of Mr. Daniels' sister's seduction, and as later material bore out, also as a repetition of the violent beatings inflicted on the patient by his stepfather.

DREAMS AND EMOTIONAL ADAPTATION

We can see, then, that the patient's conscious mind was preoccupied with an issue very different from the one that concerned his deep unconscious mind. The conscious issue was social rejection, whereas the deep unconscious issue was that of a frame-violating fee increase. And Mr. Daniels' experience of the fee increase was perceived in ways that, had they been conscious, would have disrupted his functioning, created havoc for himself and his therapist, and, in all likelihood, threatened retaliation.

The evolved capacity for deep unconscious experience enabled this patient to remain relatively calm and to stay in the counseling relationship. Yet this entailed a price because, first, the patient was staying with a counselor who had been assaultive on some level and undoubtedly would, in his ignorance of deep unconscious experience and trigger decoding, be assaultive through other interventions and frame breaks in the future. Second, driven by this deep unconscious experience to make use of displacement, Mr. Daniels acted out destructively against his employer when he refused the patient's request for a raise. Denial, repression, and the absence of deep insight protect us from emotional disequilibrium, but they do so at great cost to our emotional lives.

Summing Up

1. Triggers are the evocative stimuli that prompt emotional adaptive responses.
    a. The conscious meanings of triggers inspire conscious adaptive responses that are reflected in manifest dream contents.
    b. The unconscious meanings of triggers prompt deep

The Triggers for Dreams

unconscious adaptive responses that are reflected in the encoded meanings of dreams.

2. The manifestly perceived meanings of triggers involve a wide range of emotional conflicts and concerns related to survival, companionship, self-protection, nurturing, reproductive success (in adults), and the like. These tasks are the responsibility of the cognitive mind and the conscious system of the emotion-processing mind.

3. The unconsciously perceived meanings of triggers are centered around rules, settings, boundaries, and frames. The task of dealing with these issues has fallen to the deep unconscious system of the emotion-processing mind.

    a. When frames are violated or modified, the deep unconscious experience is that of trauma, invasion, assault, and harm, with resultant predatory death anxieties.

    b. When frames are secured, the resultant enclosure is experienced deeply unconsciously as inherently supportive and constructive, but the sense of entrapment arouses existential death anxieties.

    c. It is these trigger-related meanings that patients encode in dream images in response to frame-related triggers from their therapists.

Humans, including both patients and therapists, live in two worlds. One is directly linked to awareness. The other is never directly experienced, linked to awareness only via encoded images, and known consciously only through the use of trigger decoding. They are very different worlds of experience, vul-

133

nerability, wisdom, and coping. This basic split in the emotion-processing mind apparently has enabled humans to survive as a species, but it is as well a primary factor in human maladaptation and suffering. It also accounts for the very different domains touched on by the manifest and encoded meanings to be found in dreams and associations to dreams.

With this in mind, let's turn to the manifest dream and see what we can learn about patients and their therapists and psychotherapies from the contents and functions of the surface of patients' dreams.

CHAPTER EIGHT

The Manifest Contents of Dreams

- The manifest dream complex created by the surface contents of dreams and associations to dream elements
- Using this complex to interpret adaptive responses to the conscious meanings of known emotionally charged triggering events
- Exploring the four main areas of meaning and potential insight conveyed in manifest dream complexes

I have established a link between the manifest contents of dreams and the operations of the conscious system of the emotion-processing mind. In sum, the manifest contents of dreams reflect human efforts to cope with emotional life via adaptive responses to consciously recognized emotionally charged triggering events and their known or readily appreciated meanings.

There are several additional perspectives to keep in mind as we begin our study of this level of dreamwork. First, when I refer now to the manifest dream, I will be alluding to the dream as dreamed plus the surface contents of all associations to the dream—the manifest dream complex. As noted, manifest associations to dream elements are latent to the dream images, but they are directly stated and, therefore, belong to

135

the realm of conscious experience and processing. When they are narrative in form, these associations also encode experiences from the deep unconscious part of the mind, much as does the manifest dream itself; access to that level of meaning requires trigger decoding (see Chapter 10).

Second, we want to be clear that dreams serve two basic functions in efforts to understand the human mind and its adaptations. They are in and of themselves filled with meaning. But as a form of narrative, they also are unique creations of the human mind that are formed through a deep unconscious process of multiple representation and condensation. This means that every dream image is fashioned unconsciously to represent a large number of conscious and unconscious perceptions and reactive fantasies that have been evoked by a similarly large number of emotionally charged triggering events. Human emotional life is such that each day the mind is compelled to adapt to an enormous number of disturbing psychological and physical experiences. And as we have seen, dreams have evolved as messengers that condense multiple responses to these multiple triggers in order to make them available for *extraction* (manifest meanings) and *decoding* (encoded meanings).

Dreams are dreamed and recalled in order to reveal aspects of emotional issues that cannot be appreciated in most other ways. But dreams also are dreamed to be nodal points for a variety of associated images that even more tellingly reveal the secrets of emotional life.

Third, there is a critical difference between narrative associations to manifest dream images and those that are descriptive, explanatory, and intellectualized. In general, the intellectualized type of association and its interpretation have little power to convey truly cogent unconscious factors in, and

The Manifest Contents of Dreams

thereby insightfully modify, emotional maladaptations. They involve intellectual or pseudo-insights that have little impact on the mind and life of a patient. On the other hand, interpretations derived from the trigger decoding of narrative images of a dream and associated stories tend to have considerable power, and when unconsciously validated, have strong, curative effects on patients' maladaptations.

Whether dealing with manifest or encoded meanings, the scope of dreamwork is widened and deepened through narrative associations. These associations tend to be more powerful and meaningful than the manifest dream itself. On every level, associations to a dream are an invaluable part of dreamwork; together with the dream as dreamed and recalled, they fashion a manifest content dream complex and an encoded dream complex of considerable richness.

Fourth and last, the events that stimulate the manifest dream and its themes are almost always available to awareness (this is less often the case with triggers that evoke a dream's encoded themes). That is, both patient and therapist are likely to be aware of the emotionally charged triggering events that have prompted a manifest dream complex. This makes work with this level of meaning relatively straightforward; the trigger is readily identified and the themes are easily linked to their triggering events to yield a measure of superficial understanding and insight.

A Clinical Illustration

Stella Archer, a single woman of 23 with a severe depression, was in psychotherapy with Enid Hall, a psychiatrist. About six months into the therapy, the patient's mother suffered a

DREAMS AND EMOTIONAL ADAPTATION

mild stroke and was hospitalized. On the night of the hospitalization, Ms. Archer had a dream, which she reported in her next therapy session.

> She dreamed that she was in a hospital waiting room. Her father arrived and told her that no one was to know, but her brother had contracted AIDS. Then she was alone on a hospital unit looking for her mother's room. A nurse came to tell her that her mother had died. She awoke from the dream feeling anxious and depressed.

Ms. Archer immediately went into a description of her mother's sudden illness—her collapsing at a friend's house, being taken to the hospital, being in a coma for a short while, and coming out of the coma to find that the right side of her face and the left side of her body were paralyzed. Despite reassurances from the doctors that recovery of function was likely and that her mother's life was not in danger, the patient was worried that her mother would die. Her father had died two years earlier of pancreatic cancer. He had been a generous and loving man; his death was a terrible loss for the patient and her mother. It was around that time that Ms. Archer's depression had begun.

The nurse in the dream reminded the patient of a private nurse they had hired to take care of her father during his last days. The nurse liked to talk about other patients who had been in her care, and, on one occasion, she had described a young man who supposedly was dying of cancer, whereas the truth was that he had AIDS. Ms. Archer suddenly realized, to her suprise, that the nurse was talking about someone she had known through her work as a advertising executive. "No secret is safe these days," was her next comment in the session.

As far as Ms. Archer knew, her brother wasn't ill, but several weeks earlier he had arranged a date for her with a man

The Manifest Contents of Dreams

who was so angry, mean-spirited, and erratic that she refused to see him again. A few weeks later, her brother reported that the man had been murdered gangland style. She had experienced an uncomfortable feeling that he deserved to die. At times, her mother could be nasty and disagreeable, even violent and irrational, but Ms. Archer said that she certainly didn't want her to die.

There was more to this session, but we now have sufficient material for the present discussion.

The main consciously known trigger for this manifest dream complex (i.e., the dream itself and the associations to the dream) is, of course, the illness of Ms. Archer's mother. This is a manifestly represented (i.e., directly mentioned), consciously recognized, traumatic triggering event that is external to the therapy. In general, for patients in psychotherapy, this type of life-threatening trauma is worked over by the conscious system of the emotion-processing mind, with little deep unconscious activity. Thus, almost all of the relevant material is manifest or implied in the manifest contents, be it of the dream or associations to the dream, or any other narrative communication. Such was the case with Ms. Archer.

The dream itself indicates that the serious illness suffered by her mother had, for Ms. Archer, brought up the death of her father and her relationship with her brother, past and present. The manifest dream can be viewed as reflecting either a concern and fear that her mother might die, or as a wish that she would do so, or both. There is a theme of secrets and of criminality, and we might wonder how this pertains to the patient's mother—had she violated a law or a moral precept? Had she, for example, had an extramarital affair? Such an incident may well be superficially encoded in the story about the man Ms. Archer dated: he was a criminal who had broken the law and was killed (punished?) because of it.

It turned out that her mother had had an extramarital affair when the patient was 15 years old, something that Ms. Archer recalled later in this session. At that point, the therapist might have suggested that Ms. Archer's (thinly disguised) story about the man she had dated suggests that her mother's illness had aroused in the patient punitive death wishes against her mother for her violation of her marriage vows and betrayal of her husband and daughter. This interpretation is supported by the associations that directly connect the man to her mother—both were nasty and erratic individuals.

Finally, the patient's anxiety and depression appear to be connected to the illness of her mother. It could then be suggested that some of the patient's symptoms stem from her unconscious death wishes toward her mother—and, in the past, toward her father.

As we can see, there is much to mine from a manifest dream complex. There is, however, a notable measure of uncertainty to the speculations and interpretations made on this basis. Impressions that simply restate manifest contents tend to be simplistic and nondynamic, whereas those based on inferences made from such contents always involve ideas constructed by the therapist. They are open to error and, therefore, in need of subsequent encoded validation before a therapist can feel assured of the accuracy and cogency of this type of formulation and interpretation.

As an aside, we should recognize that, in addition to the outside trigger, there is an active, frame-related triggering event within this psychotherapy. We could develop clues to its identity by extracting the themes of the manifest dream complex. The main frame-related theme is to be found in the story about Ms. Archer's father's nurse: she had violated a patient's confidentiality and revealed a forbidden secret. There also is the allusion to lying, a theme that usually is

The Manifest Contents of Dreams

connected with a frame violation because frame breaks universally are perceived unconsciously as dishonest, deceptive, and criminal in nature. In addition, the power themes are those of murder, death, and illness; no matter how realistic a narrative tale, it always is told in a selective fashion that is shaped by unconscious triggers.

We are thus seeking a triggering event that is frame modifying and that has had powerfully destructive deep unconscious effects on this patient. Its main feature is some kind of violation of confidentiality, which directs us to look for that type of frame break by Dr. Hall.

It turns out that two weeks earlier, before she mother had suffered her stroke, the patient's mother had called Dr. Hall. She asked for a progress report on the status of her daughter's therapy, which the mother was paying for, and threatened to stop the treatment unless she received a response. Fearful of an abrupt termination, Dr. Hall had spoken briefly, positively, and in generalities about Ms. Archer's therapy to her mother.

In the session after the telephone call, Dr. Hall explained what had happened and the patient indicated consciously that she felt that her therapist had done the right thing—her mother had been having doubts about the therapy and would have stopped it if the therapist had done otherwise. Stories that followed, of betrayal and gang rape, and of a pimp who supported his prostitutes' drug habits, were not, however, interpreted in light of these frame-violating triggers: the background trigger of the therapist's accepting the mother's payment of the patient's fee and the foreground trigger of the therapist's participation in the telephone call (triggers for patients in therapy always pertain to their therapists' interventions).

The therapist's acceptance of the fee from the patient's mother permitted a third party to enter the therapy and vi-

141

Dreams and Emotional Adaptation

olated the one-to-one relationship between the patient and therapist; it also set the stage for the telephone-call deviation that followed. Further, Dr. Hall's failure to intervene regarding these deviations and the unconscious perceptions that they had evoked in the patient help to account for the intensity of this material and for Ms. Archer's continuing to work over both of these triggering interventions on the deep unconscious level.

Focusing here on the immediate frame-breaking telephone call, the dream themes indicate that Ms. Archer's unconscious perception of this frame-deviant trigger was that it was a betrayal of trust and a violation of the privacy of her therapy—a sick act, nasty and erratic, criminally murderous, and deserving of punishment in kind. These kinds of intense perceptions are characteristic of deep unconscious experience and they are entirely divorced from the patient's conscious thoughts. The unconscious experience of this trigger also had no evident direct effect on the patient's behavior toward her therapist; it is deep unconscious knowledge that was unable to lead to constructive, conscious adaptive responses.

As I have indicated, the effects of this type of unconscious perception of a therapist are usually displaced onto someone else. In this case, Ms. Archer had flown into a violent rage when a close friend at work had violated a minor confidence. The effects of deep unconscious experience are not expressed directly, but are displaced onto others with whom the unconsciously motivated behavior is quite inappropriate and maladaptive.

The Manifest Contents of Dreams

The Therapeutic Value of Manifest Contents

What then about the main areas of information and meaning that can be ascertained through explorations of manifest-content dream complexes?

Extractions of meaning from the surface of a dream can be organized into and yield information about four basic categories of concern:

1. The patient's adaptations to known triggers.
2. The patient's emotional self—his or her inner mental (intrapsychic) state, means of relating, conflicts, issues, emotionally charged choices, ego strengths and weaknesses, superego stirrings, instinctual drives needs, and the like.
3. The patient's views of life situations and of those with whom he or she interacts.
4. The evident status of the psychotherapy.

The following vignette will be used in examining each of these areas.

Dorothy Gregory was in psychotherapy with Marilyn Parks, a psychologist, because she suffered from obsessions and compulsions—repetitive concerns that her children would die and that the doors to her house were not properly locked and so intruders might enter and murder her and her family. Two years into her once-weekly therapy, she began a session with a dream.

143

> She is at a farm with her friend, Sally. They're cleaning the chicken
> coop for some little chicks. A man comes along and begins to threaten
> them. He tries to climb over the fence surrounding the chicken coop.
> Sally grabs a shovel and swings it at the man. She misses him, but he
> runs away.

Mrs. Gregory went on to say that her husband wanted to have a third child. They have discussed it, but she isn't sure how she feels about it. There are reasons why she'd like to get pregnant again, she said, but children are a lot to deal with, and having two children under the age of five has been a strain. Mrs. Gregory also said that she had been thinking about returning to work and becoming pregnant would bring an end to that possibility, at least for a while. There were too many pros and cons for her to reach a satisfactory decision, even though she'd been over every angle dozens of times. For a while, she had avoided having intercourse with her husband, but she was having sex again of late and enjoying it because she now was using contraceptives.

The farm in the dream looked like the one that Sally's parents bought when they retired. As single women in their early 20s, the patient and Sally occasionally spent weekends at the farm. They were happy times, and Mrs. Gregory loved taking care of the small animals. When she was at the farm, most of her fears would evaporate; she could sleep alone at night without being terrified that someone would break into her bedroom and murder her. Oddly enough, for the first time in years, she said that she had felt safe in her own home during the past week or so.

Sally was a good friend, but she was fickle. She'd become involved with a nasty crowd of girls and turn against the patient, but she always came back. Still, she said, it's hard to trust a woman like that.

The Manifest Contents of Dreams

An incident came to mind. Soon after Sally's parents moved into the farmhouse, a disgruntled farmhand had set it on fire. The parents were trapped in their bedroom, but were rescued at the last minute. They had survived, but had suffered smoke inhalation and minor burns. It had been a terrifying experience.

With this material in mind, let's explore the four types of information we can gather from a manifest dream complex—and from all types of manifest narrative communications.

1.   The patient's adaptations to known triggers.   The main external trigger appears to be Mrs. Gregory's husband's wish to have another child (her own attitudes and feelings about this prospect are secondary adaptive issues). In processing this emotionally charged adaptive problem with her conscious mind, her thinking was repetitive and narrow in its range, and overall quite inconclusive. Conscious explorations of emotionally charged conflicts that have weighty and contradictory considerations tend to be constricted and uncertain. As we shall see, in contrast, the deep unconscious processing of a conflicted emotionally charged triggering event involves many different, but well-defined, perspectives and leads to definitive answers.

The dream itself is not directly concerned with being pregnant. There are, however, themes that are clearly related to the pregnancy problem, and they are thinly disguised in a way that speaks for superficial unconscious processing. Most of these themes are distinctly positive: they involve cleaning chicken coops and caring for small animals and feeling safe in a closed space. These images suggest that Mrs. Gregory is, on the superficial unconscious level, favorably inclined toward becoming pregnant again and that it would be a positive experience for her.

With this said, we must realize that we have not as yet accounted for the story of the fire. It may well reflect an unconscious fear of being pregnant and the experience of a prior trauma connected with pregnancy. On the manifest level, Dr. Parks might make note of that story to Mrs. Gregory and suggest that while her images in the main speak favorably for her getting pregnant, the story of the entrapping fire may well indicate deeper anxieties that are having an unfavorable effect in this regard.

With some further effort, it might be possible to unearth related background information. In this case, Mrs. Gregory's mother had had a miscarriage when the patient was six years old and the experience had left the patient with intense unconscious fears of pregnancy. These manifest anxieties had disappeared during her adolescence, but had been replaced by obsessions and rituals, which appear to have been, in part, disguised expressions of both the miscarriage and the patient's responsive perceptions and fantasies. Still, were the memory of her mother's miscarriage eventually to reach awareness directly, it would have emerged from the superficial unconscious memory-storage subsystem and be part of conscious system thinking. In contrast, the recall of a traumatic event, or aspects of its meanings, stored in the deep unconscious memory-storage subsystem always takes place through encoded themes that must be trigger decoded to recapture or reconstruct consciously the deeply repressed incident.

As for the manifest and easily decoded material, with a single exception, it speaks favorably with regard to Mrs. Gregory's getting pregnant, far more so than did her direct ruminations about the problem. Thus, a superficial interpretation of the patient's manifest dream complex could help her get in touch with the positive aspects of her view of this possibility

The Manifest Contents of Dreams

and recognize that this is her predominant feeling. In addition, her accessible anxieties about pregnancy also could be explored through further associations to the farmhouse and, once recalled, there could be a direct exploration of the early trauma with her mother.

In advising the use of this interpretation, we must note again the many uncertainties that are inherent in manifest content interventions: they are very much open to a therapist's biases and his or her unconsciously driven selection of particular meanings and the exclusion of others.

In principle, then, manifest dream material, including themes that are thinly disguised, can be used by therapists to identify and evaluate a patient's conscious responses to known emotionally charged triggers. Outside of therapy, these triggers may involve major traumas, such as a severe illness or death; a wide range of emotionally loaded life decisions; a variety of interpersonal conflicts; and anything else with a known emotional charge.

Within therapy, a recognized trigger will involve the conscious experience of an intervention made by the therapist. The acknowledged trigger can be anything that the therapist has or has not said or done that the patient consciously feels is of some import, be it constructive or destructive. Patients' conscious assessments and responses to such triggers are, however, highly varied and inconsistent. They are notoriously unreliable, likely to serve defense far more than insight, personally biased, and inclined unconsciously toward self-harm and desperate forms of protection against death anxiety. These comments and evaluations, therefore, should not be accepted by therapists unless they obtain encoded validation, which seldom is the case (see below).

The key to working effectively with manifest contents is,

then, identifying the triggers that are most important *consciously* for a given patient. When working on this level, a therapist should try to avoid undue bias and the projection of his or her own issues and preferences onto the patient. Triggers that are mentioned directly and that then organize and give meaning to the manifest and thinly disguised dream images are most likely to belong in this category and lend themselves to weakly validated interpretations by the therapist.

2.   The patient's emotional self.   This refers to his or her inner mental (intrapsychic) state, means of relating, conflicts, issues, emotionally charged choices, ego strengths and weaknesses, superego stirrings, instinctual drives needs, symptom picture, and the like.

Conscious reactions to known triggers are immediate adaptive responses that reveal much about the patient's inner mental state and modes of relating. The triggers on which a given patient focuses, and the responsive manifest material from the patient, make it possible to glean from a manifest dream complex the status of a patient's basic mental structures and his or her coping and relating strategies. Assessments can be made of the capacities of, and issues pertaining to, the structural components of the patient's mind: the id (e.g., sexual and aggressive drives and needs); superego and ego ideal (e.g., conscience, ideals, goals, self, and self-regulation); and ego (e.g., defenses, relating, managing id and superego pressures and both intrapsychic and interpersonal conflicts, and adapting consciously to the external world).

Based on personal and theoretical preferences, a given therapist will use particular categories for appraising a patient's behaviors and mental state, and for deciding which issues and features he or she believes to be uppermost at a given interlude in the therapy. In the case of Mrs. Gregory, there is, for

The Manifest Contents of Dreams

example, an allusion to her avoiding sex with her husband, an indication of a sexual conflict. But the patient went on to say that the problem, whose main manifest source was her issues about becoming pregnant, had been resolved. This resolution implies that the patient had worked out some of her conflicts in this area.

The aggressive images in the manifest dream complex are less controlled and more conflicted. The strongest assaultive image is that of a blatant act of destruction and a virtual attempt at murder—the farmhand's setting fire to the farmhouse. This image could be taken as a conscious perception of others (see below), but it also might be a projection of aggressive impulses within the patient. In addition, there is the menacing man who appears in the manifest dream, an image that has similar implications. Based on this material, and in light of its trigger, we might speculate that Mrs. Gregory has destructive and murderous wishes that are directed at either her husband for wanting to impregnate her or the anticipated fetus.

There are other aspects of Mrs. Gregory's emotional state and relatedness that also can be extracted from this manifest dream complex. We see positive functioning in her dreaming of caring for the chicks and in her thoughts about getting pregnant and going to work. Although conflict is present, both are constructive images. There are additional caretaking images and a reference to a diminution of her symptoms when at the farm and recently at home. Also positive is Sally's ability in the dream to drive away the menacing man—an indication of the patient's own ego strengths and effective defenses. The crime of setting fire to the house implies a pathological or lax superego with poor impulse control.

As for Mrs. Gregory's primary emotional symptoms, there are two manifest references to their current status: the positive change from avoiding intercourse with her husband to engaging in it, and her feelings of safety at home of late. There also is the allusion to being symptom-free at the farm, a hopeful encoded theme that may or may not be accompanied by actual symptomatic improvement.

A great deal of present-day therapeutic work is carried out on the level of the manifest dream complex. It is essential, however, not to consider such efforts to be inherently correct or valid. Interventions made on this basis need to be subjected to some type of conscious confirmation, however uncertain, and to the more reliable encoded, deep unconscious form of validation. Unconsciously confirmed interventions based on manifest content images are quite the exception, but such efforts nevertheless may help patients to resolve aspects of their emotional maladaptations.

3. The patient's views of life situations and of those with whom he or she interacts. The dream complex alludes to menacing and violent men, and this may be linked to Mrs. Gregory's reluctance to become pregnant. There is a different picture of women: Sally drives the menacer away and is a good friend, although fickle. There also is the safety of the farm, yet the danger of being trapped and injured or killed there. In all, the manifest dream complex suggests a negative and conflicted view of men and a more positive view of women. These attitudes may well be superficially unconscious and their interpretation could be of some help to the patient, especially when organized around active triggering events.

4. The evident status of the psychotherapy. Patients do, from time to time, talk directly about their therapies and therapists, and even dream manifestly about them as well. Therapists working on this level of expression need to explore

The Manifest Contents of Dreams

the ramifications of these comments and their sources. Conscious praise of a therapist may be a positive sign, but it must be taken with a large grain of salt. It has been found clinically that, as a rule, such comments are offered by patients as an idealizing defense against their very opposite picture of the therapist on the level of deep unconscious perception. Almost always they are efforts consciously to deny the effects of a deeply unconsciously hurtful intervention. Again and again, the conscious system is invested more in defensive deception than in the truth.

In this regard, an important role is played by the tendency of conscious and deep unconscious experiences to be at opposite poles with regard to assessments of therapists' interventions. A therapist's acknowledgment of a patient's positive surface impressions of a therapy is risky and best avoided; most of the seemingly helpful effects reported by a patient come from using surface thinking to defend against and obliterate the patient's deep unconscious experience of the therapist.

In using manifest dream material for an assessment of the current status of a psychotherapy, the therapist also should be alert for images and themes that indirectly allude to therapy, including thinly disguised allusions to the treatment situation and the therapist. In contrast to work on the encoded level, which requires the identification of specific triggering events, work with manifest dream complexes tends to pertain to the general status of a given therapy and the overall efforts of the therapist. The resultant conscious evaluations, therefore, tend to be broad rather than specific, and are far less useful than deep unconscious assessments.

Comments that are critical of a therapist's intervention often contain a measure of directly stated truth, but more important, they often serve both to encode and to deny more compelling criticisms of a different intervention that are disguised in these remarks and in other narratives and dreams.

To illustrate these ideas, the caretaking imagery in Mrs. Gregory's dream indirectly suggests a positive experience of the therapist and therapy, whereas Sally's ability to drive away the menacing man seems to indicate that effective work is being done vis-à-vis the patient's emotional problems and her negative perceptions of men. The fact that these impressions are encoded, although thinly so, speaks for their likely truth value. Nevertheless, note must be made that, for the moment, they are being decoded in general terms rather than as specific encoded responses to a definitive intervention by Dr. Parks (see below).

The change from sexual abstinence to sexual activity also is a positive sign and may reflect a therapeutic gain, as may the positive images of being at the farm with Sally and being relatively symptom-free at the farm and now at home. The main indirect indications of possible problems in the therapy are the allusions to the menacing man, Sally's fickleness, and the story of the man who set fire to the farmhouse. Sally's parents did, however, escape serious harm, so the story suggests danger or harm accompanied by survival, rather than utter disaster—another possible indication of progress in the therapy.

Overall, indirect dream-related clues to the status of a psychotherapy or interventions by a therapist have limited reliability and should be checked carefully via the subsequent encoded images from the patient. Paradoxically, patient assessments that are manifestly positive tend mainly to serve maniclike denial defensiveness, whereas negative evaluations tend to be accurate. Still, exceptions to these trends do occur and therapists should turn to trigger decoding for clarification.

The Manifest Contents of Dreams

A Useful Overview

The manifest dream complex—the surface dream, the images directly conveyed in associations to the dream, and thinly disguised narrative themes—is a good place for a therapist to begin his or her assessment of the many facets of consciously accessible emotional adaptations, a patient's inner mental world and modes of relatedness, and the symptom picture. It is especially valuable to develop manifest-level formulations that are organized around known adaptive issues and triggers so that a fundamental adaptive position is sustained; the adaptive viewpoint is, as noted, both basic and most meaningful emotionally.

Nevertheless, therapists should realize that there is a second level of meaning to every manifest dream; it is reflected in the encoded dream complex. The decision as to whether to expand one's purview and therapeutic power by also working with deep unconscious meaning and experience is one that every therapist must make. We will soon turn to the techniques involved, but for now, consider the following repressed trigger so that we can compare and contrast the two levels of emotional experience and psychotherapeutic efforts.

The Repressed Trigger

On reviewing this material for themes that could act as a bridge to a ground rule of psychotherapy, can we suggest a possible missing within-therapy triggering event that may have prompted the encoded aspects of this dream complex?

There are several clues to the nature of the missing trigger, which we expect to be frame related because the ground rules of therapy attract the sensitivities of the deep unconscious system. The primary clues are these: caretaking (a positive theme suggesting a constructive ground-rule intervention); keeping the menacing man out of the chicken coop and getting rid of him (sustaining a secured frame and eliminating a threat to violate that frame—getting rid of an intruder, a third party); and the image of being trapped in a fire and nearly dying. (In addition to their strongly positive attributes, secured frames are experienced deeply unconsciously as entrapping and evocative of existential death anxiety [Langs, 1996b, 1997, 1998b].) As a group, these themes suggest a frame-securing intervention by Dr. Parks that involved preventing a menacing third party from entering Mrs. Gregory's therapy space and becoming involved in her therapy.

The actual triggering event was a call from Mrs. Gregory's internist, who had seen the patient for an office visit and was concerned about her mental state because of evident psychosomatic symptoms. The internist had asked the therapist for information, but Dr. Parks simply said that she wouldn't even acknowledge that Mrs. Gregory was her patient. She informed the internist that she did not discuss patients with third parties under any circumstances and that she hoped that he would understand her position. In the following session, the hour before the one we are exploring, the therapist had told the patient what had happened.

This frame-securing trigger had evoked in Mrs. Gregory a compelling deep unconscious perception of her therapist in light of the intervention. These impressions were selectively experienced and are reflected in the encoded material. They suggest the following. The internist had tried to intrude, but Dr. Parks had kept him from entering the therapeutic space and had chased him away from where he didn't belong,

The Manifest Contents of Dreams

thereby providing the patient with protection. This was a positive caretaking and friendly intervention, and it was the deep unconscious basis for Mrs. Gregory's being able to resolve her sexual conflicts and resume sex with her husband, and to experience some relief from her symptoms.

Nevertheless, with the frame secured, the patient also experienced a burst of existential death anxiety and a fear of entrapment and annihilation, which, however, she was able to contain and limit. The mixture of positive and negative themes—the latter death-related and entrapping—is typical of communications from patients who undergo a frame-securing intervention by a psychotherapist.

We can see that decoding the encoded meanings of a dream complex yields a very different and far more specific picture of this patient—her emotional issues and adaptive resources— than that at which we arrive by looking only at the manifest dream contents.

Summing Up

1. Manifest dreams and the manifest meanings of associations to dreams make up *the manifest content dream complex.*

2. This complex reflects the adaptive efforts of the conscious system of the emotion-processing mind in response to consciously identified triggers and their consciously recognized meanings.

    a. As such, this dream complex is of value as a source of superficial interpretations of conscious concerns and their evident or superficial unconscious ramifications.

3. The four basic categories of meaning and concern that

can be illuminated through an understanding of the manifest dream complex are:

a. The patient's conscious adaptations to consciously recognized triggering events.

b. The patient's consciously knowable emotional self and the status of his or her conscious coping abilities.

c. The patient's conscious view of his or her life situation and of important others.

d. The consciously appreciated status of the psychotherapy.

4. While yielding superficial insights, these conscious appraisals may be at variance with deep unconscious appraisals. Of the two, the latter are always the more reliable and accurate reflection of the emotional realities with which a patient is dealing.

CHAPTER NINE

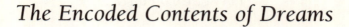

The Encoded Contents of Dreams

- Clarifying the technique of trigger decoding
- Exploring the realm of deep unconscious experience
- The interplay between triggers (external reality) and themes (internal adaptive response)
- The role of the thematic contents of dreams in the development of adaptation-oriented interpretations
- The process of linking themes to their evocative triggers in order to provide patients with deep unconscious insights and frame-securing interventions

There is a distinct discontinuity between the realms of conscious and deep unconscious experience. As a result, there is a related discontinuity between manifest dream complexes and their superficial unconscious, readily decoded images, on the one hand, and encoded dream complexes and their difficult-to-decode images, on the other. And finally, there also is a discontinuity between manifest content and trigger-decoding forms of psychotherapy. Yet, regardless of whether or not a therapist intends to use trigger decoding to access deep unconscious experience and processing, it is essential to understand how this part of the mind operates and influences emotional behavior. The deep unconscious system is by far the most powerful determinant of the tribulations of emotional life.

Trigger Decoding

Trigger decoding is, as noted, the basic therapeutic technique used to access deep unconscious experience and adaptive processing. In essence, this activity requires:

1. Identifying the active, within therapy, emotionally charged, triggering event—the therapeutic intervention—that has prompted the patient's encoded, deep unconscious responses. In most instances, the intervention is frame-related.

2. Formulating the most compelling universal meanings of the triggering intervention and developing a sense of the meanings to which the patient is most likely to be selectively sensitive.

3. Decoding the themes in the patient's encoded dream complex and treating them as reflections of the patient's personally selected, valid unconscious perceptions of the activating triggering event.

4. Taking into account the patient's deep unconscious processing of these unconsciously perceived meanings and recognizing the patient's reactions to these perceptions, including the deep unconscious system's proposed adaptive solutions.

5. Integrating these formulations into a one- or two-part intervention by linking the encoded themes to their triggers:

    a. An *interpretation* of the patient's material is offered as an explanatory narrative of adaptation that is used to identify the unconscious basis for a

The Encoded Contents of Dreams

patient's currently active maladaptations, such as symptoms, interpersonal difficulties, and resistances.

The model interpretation is the result of a completed trigger-decoding process. It stresses the patient's valid, personally selected, unconscious perceptions of the therapist as a result of a particular comment or action. It is structured in the following manner.

> I [the therapist] did such and such [alluding to a manifestly represented trigger that usually is a frame-related intervention, securing or modifying a ground rule], and you [the patient] unconsciously experienced this and that meaning in what I did [referring to the encoded dream themes as unconsciously perceived]. As a result of these unconscious perceptions, you experienced this or that symptom or resistance or symptom alleviation [explaining the deep unconscious basis for symptomatic change, much of it depending on whether the frame has been modified or secured].

When the material permits, connections are made to figures and events in the patient's outside life, including those from his or her early childhood, as they relate to the deep unconscious experience at hand.

b. When dealing with a frame-modifying intervention, the interpretation is, if at all possible, accompanied by an actual *frame-securing intervention*. This is done by using the patient's encoded directives as a guide; consistently, they point toward the rectification of modified ground rules and to sus-

DREAMS AND EMOTIONAL ADAPTATION

taining secured frames. Thus, with frame-deviant triggers, dreamwork should lead to both interpretation and frame-management efforts, and both should obtain subsequent encoded validation.

From the adaptive vantage point, every intervention pertaining to the deep unconscious system must begin with an environmental triggering event, almost always one that occurred within the therapy and is frame-related. The interpretation starts with a currently active trigger and thereby inherently touches on the patient's immediate emotion-processing efforts and is relevant to the patient's current emotional life.

Once the adaptive core of a patient's deep unconscious experience has been interpreted, genetic connections, unconsciously driven symptomatic acts, resistances, affects, intrapsychic fantasies, and both conscious and encoded memories can be interpreted, depending on their availability in the patient's material. An interpretation based on trigger decoding appears to be the most complete effort a therapist can make to enable a patient truly to comprehend the unconscious basis of his or her emotional adaptations and issues and so achieve symptom resolution.

Deep Unconscious Experience

A summary of the main features of deep unconscious experience and adaptive efforts will enable us to turn to the details of the trigger decoding of dreams with a reasonable sense of where we are and what we are trying to accomplish.

The key features of deep unconscious experience are:

The Encoded Contents of Dreams

1. Intake involves the unconscious perceptions of personally selected, anxiety-provoking meanings of environmental triggering events.
   a. Because it is relatively nondefensive, unconscious perception is more in touch with reality than is conscious perception.
2. There is a strong sensitivity to triggers related to boundaries, rules, and frames, and a consistent preference for secured frames.
3. There is, as well, a great sensitivity to explicit and implicit predatory threats of harm, physical and emotional, and to existential death issues.
4. The deep unconscious system has very adept adaptive capacities and a superb intelligence for the processing of incoming information and meaning, and the system consistently reaches wise and health-giving solutions to activated adaptive issues.
5. Output from the system is never direct and undisguised, but always requires encoded narratives.
6. Conscious access to deep unconscious experience and adaptive responses is, therefore, feasible only via trigger decoding.
7. By design, and reinforced by the effects of personal traumas and unconsciously shared social preferences, there is a strong defensive need in all humans to remain unaware of deep unconscious contents and experiences.
8. Because the deep unconscious system processes some of the most unbearable aspects of emotional life (individual and collective), trigger decoding is an especially difficult therapeutic task. Critical triggers and powerful meanings of known triggers often are missed consciously (obliterated, denied, and repressed) by patients and/or their therapists. In addition, patients show var-

ious degrees of resistance to generating the narrative themes that encode their unconsciously perceived meanings of triggers. Both they and their therapists also may demonstrate a great reluctance to engage in the trigger-decoding process because it will reveal painful and forbidding deep unconscious experiences. And when they do attempt to do so, they often will fail properly to link encoded dream themes to their most compelling triggers.

Thus, both patients and therapists have a built-in tendency to avoid the conscious articulation of deep unconscious experience, as well as an opposition to carrying out the trigger-decoding process that can bring this critical level of emotional experience to the conscious mind.

Clarifying Trigger Decoding: A Vignette

George Matthews, 30 years of age, was in psychotherapy with Kathleen Dunne, a social worker. His primary complaint was that he had a violent temper that he often was unable to control; it had cost him several good jobs as a computer programmer and had wreaked havoc with his marriage of two years.

With regard to his therapy, two weeks before the first session to be described here, which took place about six months into his treatment, Ms. Dunne had increased her patient's reduced fee from $50 to $75 per session.

The patient came to the session feeling very upset and suicidal. He had quarreled with his wife, flown into a rage, and uncharacteristically had hit her. She had left their apartment

The Encoded Contents of Dreams

to stay with a friend and had threatened divorce. As the session unfolded, it was focused mainly on the quarrel, which had been set off by his wife's asking for extra money to meet unexpected household expenses. The patient and therapist explored the question of why Mr. Matthews had such poor impulse control, and they connected the problem to his father's having been an alcoholic who often flew into rages and beat his wife and children.

Toward the end of the session, Mr. Matthews became furious with Ms. Dunne because nothing had been resolved. He refused to end his session out of fear that he might harm himself after leaving the therapist's office. Concerned about her patient's suicidal ideation, the therapist told Mr. Matthews that she could extend the session 15 minutes, but would have to charge him for the extra time. He agreed with her plan, and then spoke of his anger at "grabby" women who try to exploit men, and of his mistrust of his wife, who, he said, probably bought herself unneeded clothes with the extra money he gave her. In the additional time allotted, Mr. Matthews did calm down, and as the session was nearing its new end, he thanked his therapist for being responsive to his needs and for extending his hour.

Mr. Matthews began the next session by handing Ms. Dunne a check for his previous month's sessions, which included the extended previous session and two sessions at her new fee. He asked if the check was for the right amount as he was a little confused by the fee increase and by having to pay for the extra time at the last session. Ms. Dunne examined the check and said that it was correct, and Mr. Matthews thanked her again for extending the previous hour. He had felt a lot better, he said, although the next day he had had a fight with his boss, who wanted him to work overtime. He then reported a brief dream.

> He is standing on a pile of dirt looking at a fast-moving river.

The pile of dirt brought to his mind two newspaper stories. The first was about a local engineer who was part of a team building an apartment house. The project was nearly completed when the engineer noticed that dirt was sinking away from the building's foundation. He realized that it needed reinforcement lest the building collapse and people be injured or killed. He arranged for the necessary measures to be taken despite the considerable extra cost involved.

The second story concerned a man who had been buried alive in a coffin by two men who were holding him captive for ransom. When the money was paid, the kidnappers disappeared, and it was only by luck that a teenager had spotted the odd-looking dirt pile and had dug a little way down to find the coffin and the man. When he was freed, the first thing the man said was that the incident led him to appreciate the good things in life.

Mr. Matthews said he felt that this was the worst thing anyone could do to a person, and that he hoped that the kidnappers, who were eventually apprehended, would roast in hell. They needed to learn that you don't treat people like that.

The river in his dream reminded Mr. Matthews of a camping trip that he had taken with a girlfriend some 10 years earlier. They had hiked along a beautiful river and into some woods, but before they realized it, it began to get dark and they were unable to find their way back to their campsite. Lost in the darkness, they became cold and hungry. They huddled together, neither of them knowing what to do, each blaming the other for their predicament. They slept in the woods that night and then, with dawn, were finally able to

The Encoded Contents of Dreams

retrace their steps, only to discover that their supplies had been stolen. They later learned that another pair of lost campers had eaten the food in order to survive while searching for their own campsite. Mr. Matthews' girlfriend had contracted pneumonia as a result of the cold and he felt responsible for her illness, because, he maintained, he should have known when enough was enough.

What is the frame-modifying trigger that accounts unconsciously for Mr. Matthews' displaced rage against his wife?

We are dealing here with a narrative that is both an encoded story and a displaced acting out on the basis of a deep unconscious experience of a frame-modifying trigger—the consequences of therapists' interventions are both communicative and behavioral. As for the trigger, the bridging theme in the incident with the wife is that of money, specifically her asking for more money. This theme encodes the fee increase imposed by Ms. Dunne because she had been seeing Mr. Matthews at a lower-than-usual rate and he had been given a raise at his new job.

Consciously, the patient had seen the sensibility of the fee increase and had agreed to it. But his behavior with his wife indicates that he had a very different deep unconscious reaction to this frame-modifying triggering event, which is an unusual frame deviation that secures the frame; the intervention corrects an existing deviation (the low fee), but does so by changing the agreed-upon frame (modifying the rule of keeping the same fee for the entire course of a given therapy). The effects of this type of intervention generally tend to be mixed, but they usually include a positive experience accompanied by anxieties derived from the frame-securing aspect.

Despite the surface justification for, and conscious accep-

DREAMS AND EMOTIONAL ADAPTATION

tance of, the fee increase, the deep unconscious mind sees this type of frame change in part as a frame-deviant, endangering act—and so, in terms of this material, as exploitative and not to be trusted. The frame-securing aspects of the intervention tend not to emerge clearly until the frame-deviant qualities are interpreted and worked through with the patient. In this instance, it was the failure to interpret the patient's deep unconscious experience of the frame-modifying aspects of the therapist's intervention that most likely unconsciously motivated Mr. Matthews to act out against his wife. This type of uninterpreted repression and denial of the unconsciously perceived meanings of a frame-altering trigger generally leads patients to carry out displaced, destructive symptomatic acts whose deep unconscious sources tend to go unrecognized.

Although this patient consciously accepted the fee increase and gave it little further thought, he continued to process its frame-deviant, greedy and intrusive, qualities deeply unconsciously, and acted out against his wife on this basis. Many frame-related interventions, whether securing or deviating from ground rules, are quickly dropped by the conscious mind, but continue to be worked over by the deep unconscious mind, as reflected in patients' encoded dreams and narratives. Had the therapist interpreted the patient's deep unconscious perception of her frame-securing frame modification, it is very likely that Mr. Matthews' symptoms would have lessened and there would have been no need to extend his hour—itself a serious additional frame modification that the therapist invoked to deal with the uninterpreted frame-related ground-rule intervention connected with the fee.

In the second session described above, the patient evidently was adapting to both an immediate and a background trigger. The former trigger for the dream material in that session was the extension of the prior session for 15 minutes. The active

The Encoded Contents of Dreams

background trigger was the fee increase. Both triggers are frame deviant, although the fee increase also was frame securing because it corrected a deviant low fee by increasing it to Ms. Dunne's usual amount.

Triggers and Themes

Triggers and themes are the two elements that are linked together to make a trigger-decoded interpretation.

Triggers

Triggers are the emotionally charged events whose meanings elicit conscious and unconscious adaptive responses, including encoded dream themes (see also Chapter 7). Some additional clinical precepts regarding triggers are:

1. For patients in psychotherapy, the main triggers to which a patient responds deeply unconsciously are therapy-related and interventional. While this includes everything of import that a therapist does and does not say or do, the most compelling triggers for the deep unconscious system are, as noted, those that pertain to the therapist's establishment and management of the setting, ground rules, and boundaries of the therapeutic situation.

2. As the activators of adaptational responses, environmental triggers are external events of great importance in one's emotional life and the primary causes of emotional maladaptations and dream formation, with the secondary causes being internal.

3. Because of the natural defenses of the conscious system, the most cogent evocative triggers and their most dis-

turbing meanings tend to be either denied and repressed or difficult to identify. The status of the ground
rules of therapy thus must be subjected to continual
monitoring by a psychotherapist in order for him or
her effectively to trigger decode a patient's material.

4. By and large, frame-modifying triggers are easier to
    work with than are those that are frame securing. This
    is mainly attributable to the finding that we are far
    more able to deal with the predatory death anxieties
    evoked by frame-altering triggers than with the existen-
    tial death anxieties produced by secured frame triggers.

5. An appreciation of the universal meanings that accrue
    to all frame-modifying and frame-securing interven-
    tions, and of the particular meanings of interventions
    related to each of the specific ground rules of therapy,
    is an essential resource for formulating the meanings
    of dream themes and moving toward their trigger de-
    coding.

6. Once an active trigger has been identified by a thera-
    pist, the first step toward trigger decoding is to deter-
    mine how the patient has alluded to that trigger, if at
    all. There are three possibilities:

    a. The trigger has been afforded a *manifest represen-
        tation*; that is, it was mentioned directly by the pa-
        tient. In his second session, Mr. Matthews, for
        example, alluded directly to Ms. Dunne's fee in-
        crease, the extra time she gave him, and the charge
        for that time.

    b. There is an *encoded allusion* to the trigger. In the
        first session, Mr. Matthews alluded to his wife's re-
        quest for some extra money, thereby fashioning an
        encoded reference to his therapist's fee increase—
        her request for more money.

The Encoded Contents of Dreams

    c.   There is *no viable allusion* to the trigger either manifestly or in encoded form.

7.   Listening to the encoded meanings of dreams and formulating them entail decoding efforts that are guided by the nature and implications of an identified interventional trigger. If, in the presence of power themes, this linking process proves to be difficult or impossible to implement, or does not obtain encoded validation, the therapist should search for another, overlooked trigger that more cogently organizes the dream themes into a meaningful deep unconscious constellation and response.

Themes

Themes are messages that reflect the conscious and, especially, the deep unconscious responses to triggers. Thus, the adaptive capacities of a patient are most clearly revealed through the images of the encoded dream complex, which must, as we have seen, be decoded in light of their evocative triggers.

Triggers evoke themes and themes encode triggers—therein lies the secret to trigger decoding.

With regard to themes, the following should be taken into account:

1.   Meaningful themes in dream complexes must be of two kinds if a patient's material is to lend itself to trigger decoding:

    a.   *Bridging themes* that connect the narrative themes to a particular, active frame-related trigger. The allusion to the request for more money in Mr. Matthews' story of his wife bridges over to, or connects with, the therapist's request for a fee increase.

169

b. *Power themes*, such as the damage package of death, illness, injury, and harm. Sexual themes also have power and usually stem from one of two sources: First, they may serve as reflections of the seductive qualities of all frame modifications. Second, they may function as sexualized, manic defenses against secured-frame, existential death anxieties. While there are no overt sexual themes in Mr. Matthews' material, there are power themes of the possibility of a building's collapsing and people being killed or injured, near-death through entrapment, criminality (kidnapping and collecting a ransom), illness (the girlfriend's pneumonia), and stealing food (however necessary for survival).

The themes of a dream complex must account, in principle, for both the nature of the trigger (what the therapist has done framewise) and its most powerful meanings (how it has affected the patient deeply unconsciously).

2. In a sense, encoded themes are always right; they are truthful and in touch with reality. Conscious thoughts and perceptions are unreliable and often deceptive; in contrast, one can depend on deep unconscious perceptions. This means that the most powerful themes in a dream complex have been evoked by a frame-related trigger and, therefore, must be meaningfully accounted for by identifying or discovering the currently active triggers to which they relate. Similarly, a therapist's conscious decision that a particular trigger is active and pertinent to the thematic material may be correct or erroneous, but a patient's powerful encoded themes always point correctly to some active triggering event.

The Encoded Contents of Dreams

The Linking Process

In looking at the surface of the dream, we realize that, by itself, the manifest dream reveals little, if anything, of note about Mr. Matthews' adaptive issues and responses. The surface images indicate that the therapist's interventions created a pile of dirt. This image may well suggest a lack of meaning to Ms. Dunne's recent efforts—a conjecture that is, of course, very general and highly speculative.

As for the surface associations to the dream (the manifest dream complex), they appear to be connected to the request for extra money by Mr. Matthew's wife. The themes can be taken as his thinly disguised feelings of entrapment in his marriage, and of his feeling that his wife was asking for some kind of ransom and misleading or deceiving him in some way.

Linking Illustrated
Without further pursuing the manifest level, how would we trigger decode this encoded dream complex considering the two unresolved triggers?

The three narrative associations to the dream are, as is typical, far more powerful and meaningful than the dream itself. The linking process calls for extracting the themes of each story and connecting them, as valid, personally selected unconscious perceptions, to the triggers that evoked the narrative themes. Following are some of the more cogent interpretations that can be made on the basis of this material.

The first interpretation derives from the story of the sinking foundation. Linking the themes in this narrative to the triggers of the fee increase and the extension of the patient's session

DREAMS AND EMOTIONAL ADAPTATION

for which an added fee was charged would lead to the following intervention.

> At the beginning of the session, you paid your fee for last month's sessions and mentioned my increasing your fee [alluding to a manifest representation of a frame-related trigger]. You then reported the dream of a pile of dirt and associated three stories to the dream image. In the first story, the dirt is connected with a defect in a frame that must be corrected lest the entire structure collapse and people be injured or killed. There is considerable cost involved, but the necessary steps are taken nonetheless.
>
> This story seems to be connected to the fee increase and to reflect your unconscious appreciation of the destructive aspects of my continuing to charge you a reduced fee—the very foundation of your therapy was impaired. The story goes on to indicate that the fee increase was a dire necessity lest the entire treatment be destroyed, harming both of us. In all, the story reveals your appreciation that the low fee was threatening the continuation of the therapy, and that the fee increase, although costly, was a sound measure to take because it would stabilize and secure the frame of the therapy.
>
> This same narrative also reveals some of your unconscious perceptions of my extending your session. This, too, was seen as a costly measure, but one that was necessary to solidify your therapy and help you to stabilize yourself so that you would not harm yourself—and me.

Both of these interpretations touch on the positive effects of two frame deviations that were invoked to secure the therapy: the need for the fee increase is much clearer than the need to extend the session, which is marginally justified by the patient's suicidal thinking and poor impulse control.

To continue the interpretation of these two triggers, the second story—about being buried alive—seems to be decod-

The Encoded Contents of Dreams

able in light of the trigger of the additional time and the added fee for that time, as follows:

> To extend our understanding of your reaction to my extending your session last week, your story about the man who was buried alive in a coffin by kidnappers who wanted his money speaks to another unconscious reaction to my decision. The images in this narrative convey an unconscious experience of being kidnapped and trapped by me in a way that threatened your life and did you harm, and of my doing so in order to take money from you illegally because I collected an additional fee for the time. You speak of what I did as a crime, and, in a sense, it was a crime for me to violate our agreement to meet for 50 minutes each session for a specified fee. Your images also indicate that you feel that I deserve to be punished for what I did and taught a lesson so I'll never do it again. Well, I have been taught that lesson. There will be no more extensions of your sessions, as adding time to your sessions is, as you are telling me unconsciously, too heinous a crime to be justified for any reason.

This interpretation touches on the frame-deviant aspects of the extension of the patient's hour. Mr. Matthews unconsciously experienced this intervention as a frame-deviant form of entrapment. (Through condensation, the same image appears also to portray the patient's feelings of being entrapped by the frame-securing qualities of Ms. Dunne's interventions, especially the rectification of the patient's frame-deviant low fee.) Most important, the patient's encoded narratives are taken as valid unconscious perceptions and the themes are used as a basis for securing the frame with regard to the ground rule that states that the therapist's fee is fixed throughout a therapy and that sessions are to last 50 minutes. With frame modifications, both interpretation and frame rectification are essential.

DREAMS AND EMOTIONAL ADAPTATION

As for the fee increase, the second story could be interpreted as follows:

> The story of the kidnapping and ransom indicates that my increasing your fee was seen as dishonest and entrapping, as life threatening. But it also secured the ground rules of therapy by bringing your fee into line with my usual fees. In that respect, the story also seems to touch on the anxieties aroused in you by my securing the ground rule regarding your fee. With the therapy frame more securely set, you seem to feel entrapped and endangered, and concerned with dying. In the end, you do survive, and you add that the change seems to have enabled you to appreciate the good things in life.

The third story associated with the dream bridges over to the immediate trigger of extending the hour and, more distantly, to the additional fee that the therapist collected—and to the fee increase, as well. It trigger decodes as follows:

> You thanked me for extending your time last session, but your story points to another, less positive unconscious view of that decision. It indicates that your unconscious experience is that the extension got us lost in the therapy and trapped you in a way that led you to feel that your life was endangered. The story also indicates your sense that I should have taken responsibility for seeing to it that you left the session on time—something I will do in the future, lest I do things that could make you ill.
>
> The allusion to stealing your food [referring to an encoded representation of one of the triggers] suggests that the added fee I collected and my recent fee increase, both of which you mentioned earlier, were justified actions, but nevertheless were ways of dishonestly taking money from you.

The Encoded Contents of Dreams

Here, too, the therapist would be both interpreting and rectifying a departure from an ideal ground rule: the extension of the patient's hour. But with all this said, the interventions would not be considered correct unless the patient subsequently provided encoded validation.

Details of the Linking Process

The final step in trigger decoding involves, as we are seeing, linking the triggers to the themes. Its most important features are:

1. It is best to begin a linking intervention with a mention of the active trigger, alluding to it either manifestly or through its best encoded representation, depending on what is available in the patient's material.
   a. With a manifest representation of the trigger in the patient's material, the therapist is able to offer a trigger-decoded interpretation. It begins with a direct reference to the trigger and then decodes the available encoded power themes as personally selected, valid unconscious perceptions of the meanings of the triggering event and the patient's experience of the therapist who intervened accordingly.
   b. An encoded representation of a trigger calls for a playback of encoded themes that begins with the theme that best bridges to and portrays in disguise the unmentioned trigger (Langs, 1992a). It then refers to the power themes that are most cogently relevant to the meanings and implications of the omitted trigger. If correct, this effort finds its optimum validation when the patient is able to resolve his or her communicative resistances and

recall the repressed, unmentioned trigger. In addition, the technical precept is, as noted, that the therapist does *not*, for any reason, mention a trigger directly that the patient has not alluded to manifestly—the patient's communicative defenses must be respected.

2. When the therapist's intervention refers to or has involved a frame modification, the patient's themes also are likely to contain encoded models of rectification or correctives—encoded instructions to the therapist as to how best to manage the ground rules of the therapy and secure the frame. These correctives call for supplementing an interpretation with rectification of the modified ground rule: both words and deeds are needed.

3. A linked, trigger-decoded intervention or frame-securing effort by a therapist cannot be deemed to be correct and constructive without receiving encoded validation in the patient's subsequent material. Confirmation usually takes the form of allusions to well-functioning individuals and positive experiences, and/or the addition of fresh encoded themes that further illuminate the therapist's intervention.

Many psychological and communicative resistances against trigger-decoded insights and secured frames are built into the architecture of the emotion-processing mind. As a result, sound trigger-decoding efforts tend initially to evoke encoded validation from patients and then to prompt subsequent resistances.

Therapists who decide to work on this level of human experience and/or to trigger decode their own dreams and nar-

The Encoded Contents of Dreams

ratives according to their personal and professional triggers will soon discover their own inevitable conflicted needs and difficulties in trying to work effectively in this deep unconscious realm. The power of the resistances directed against linking and trigger decoding, a natural feature of the emotion-processing mind, is considerable.

Summing Up

1. The adaptive approach to dreams culminates in interpretations of deep unconscious experience generated through the process of trigger decoding.
2. These efforts enable patients to understand their deep unconscious perceptions of, and adaptive processing response to, emotionally charged triggering events.
   a. Many of these traumatic or frame-securing events are repressed by patients, either in their entirety or with respect to their most compelling, anxiety-provoking meanings.
3. Trigger decoding often calls for a therapist's recognition of a patient's repressed triggers, which typically involve the therapist's frame-securing and frame-modifying interventions.
4. The themes embodied in patients' encoded dream complexes (the dream and narrative associations to its images or elements) disguise their deep unconscious experience and adaptive processing of the currently active interventions or triggers created by their therapists.
5. A meaningful pool of themes contains both bridging themes, which connect the encoded dream images to their triggers, and power themes, such as the damage package, which reveal in disguise the most compelling

meanings of patients' experiences of a relevant triggering event.

6. Trigger decoding culminates in a meaningful linking of the themes in a dream complex to their trigger(s). This type of interpretation focuses on patients' valid, but selected, unconscious perceptions of actual meanings inherent in a triggering event.

   a. As material permits, the linked interpretation is extended to an understanding of the early-life (personal genetic) relationships and traumatic events that are connected to the current triggering event and the patient's maladaptations.

   b. Most traumatic and frame-modifying triggers recreate, in some form, a version of an earlier trauma. Distortion is not a factor in deep unconscious perception and experience.

7. In all, trigger-decoded interpretations touch on the most powerful unconscious forces in emotional life and pertain to the deep structure of emotional maladaptations. Along with secured frame holding, they are a basic source of "cure."

CHAPTER TEN

Dream Psychotherapy

- Introducing dream or empowered psychotherapy, a new form of treatment designed to provide patients with maximum access to their world of deep unconscious experience
- The structure and techniques of dream psychotherapy, the self-processing exercise

The development of a strong adaptive approach to dreams and a new model of the mind has led to a new mode of psychotherapy in which dreamwork plays a pivotal role. Identified by various names, such as empowered, dream, or self-processing psychotherapy, this treatment form has been designed to reach into the deep unconscious sources of the fundamental conflicts and emotional issues, personal and universal, with which patients are faced (Langs, 1993). Its goal is to help them to resolve their interpersonal and intrapsychic emotional difficulties through the achievement of deep structural changes in the architecture of the emotion-processing mind and to replace maladaptive inclinations with a repertoire of constructive adaptive resources.

Although the primary focus of this book is on dreamwork

with patients, it is well to realize that empowered psychotherapy also is a means by which psychotherapists can engage privately in what are called *self-processing exercises* to gain access to their own worlds of deep unconscious experience and adaptation. Most of this work is best done using frame-related triggers from a therapist's own psychotherapy practice and personal life, and developing themes through the recall of current dreams and associating to their elements (for details, see Langs, 1993).

The goals of this form of psychotherapy can be achieved only when the conditions and process of therapy are fashioned in such a manner as to enable patients both to communicate the fullness of their dreams and encoded narratives and to discover their most pressing triggers. This makes it possible for the trigger-decoding process to be carried out in an optimal and most productive fashion. The therapeutic results achieved in this way are based on the development of deep unconscious insights pertaining to the therapeutic experience as they touch mainly on a patient's death-related traumas and predatory and existential death anxieties.

Death-related issues are the core unconscious adaptive problem behind both the basic design of the emotion-processing mind and the specific life problems and emotional dysfunctions with which a given patient must deal. Other conflicts, whether about one's identity, relationships with significant others, psychological self-maintenance, sexual and aggressive problems, or similar issues, constitute more superficial levels of concern. They do, of course, need to be worked over on their own turf, but an in-depth therapy must also deal with the effects of life traumas and explorations of, and insights into, a patient's adaptive and maladaptive responses to the inevitable predatory and existential death anxieties that ultimately confront all humans.

Dream Psychotherapy

The defensive design of the emotion-processing mind and individual resistances against accessing the deep unconscious realm of experience make this an exceedingly difficult undertaking in the relatively limited period of 45 or 50 minutes. By and large, much more time is needed to enable patients to generate decodable and interpretable material relating to these fundamental issues and to overcome their resistances to identifying their most compelling active trigger events. This temporal requirement, and the need for extensive and powerful narrative material and triggers, has had a great influence on the ground rules and other features of dream psychotherapy.

Structure of Dream Psychotherapy

This new treatment form can be characterized as follows:

1. The therapy has two distinct goals:
    a. To help patients to modify their emotional maladaptations through the experience of deep unconscious insight and frame-securing interventions.
    b. To enable patients to learn how to carry out self-processing exercises on their own and so have available a lasting means of enhancing their adaptive resources and resolving their emotional conflicts and dysfunctions.
2. Because of the defensive, resistance-oriented design of the emotion-processing mind, the process-related rules of this therapy are not open and unencumbered, but are well defined. There is, indeed, but a single, relatively narrow path from a manifest dream to a trigger-decoded insight, and the therapy is constructed so as

181

to afford the patient the best possible opportunity to traverse that path.

3. The therapy is built around a basic *adaptive task*, namely, that the patient begin each session with a recent dream and engage in the self-processing effort in order to arrive at a deep unconscious insight and/or model of rectification of a deviant aspect of the treatment frame. This task provides both therapist and patient with an opportunity to observe the emotion-processing mind in action, as it is engaged in active efforts at adaptation and at achieving deep unconscious insight.

4. The sessions are once a week, face-to-face, and each lasts an hour and a half.

5. Because the therapy is quasi-educational, the fee is paid in advance for segments of four sessions each.

6. The therapist sets aside the time for the patient, who has the option of renewing the four-session sequence for as long as he or she wishes.

7. The patient is given the first 40 minutes of each session in which to carry out, entirely on his or her own, a *self-processing exercise* (an adaptation-oriented form of nonintellectualized self-exploration) whose objective is to reach a significant trigger-decoded insight. The therapist is completely silent during this time.

8. The therapist is active during the remaining 50 minutes of each session, working to help the patient recognize and resolve his or her communicative resistances and to reach the deep insights that almost always elude patients; the defenses of the conscious system directed against deep unconscious experience render it all but impossible for an individual to reach meaningfully into this realm of experience on his or her own.

Dream Psychotherapy

9. Because of the massive defenses against the self-processing effort, the dreamwork in this therapy is highly structured. The natural tendency of the human mind to find ways to avoid reaching deep unconscious insight is countered by carefully defining the means by which this can be accomplished. The following are the steps in the process.

   a. *Reporting a recent dream, one dreamed since the last self-processing session.* If the patient is unable to recall a dream of this type, he or she is obligated to make up a dream equivalent—an original, brief fictional story with a beginning, middle, and end. Known as an *origination narrative*, it serves to convey encoded meaning and, more important, as a point of departure for narrative associations, so-called guided associations.

   b. *Guiding associations to the elements of the dream.* If left to freely associate, patients typically move away from encoded meaning and deep unconscious experience. To counter this tendency, they are required to turn to the elements of the original dream to think of stories that are evoked by each dream element or image. In most instances, the associated narratives involve incidents from the patient's personal life and embody themes that are more powerful than those in the original dream. The dream and associations constitute an encoded dream complex or pool of encoded themes that connect to a currently active trigger to which they will be linked.

   c. *Identifying the patient's current maladaptations and resistances—so-called self-indicators.* These are the targeted dysfunctions whose unconscious

183

motives and meanings will be explained through a completed trigger-decoding exercise. The deep insights achieved should illuminate the unconscious sources of these disturbances; they primarily are responses to unconscious perceptions of therapist-created triggers that have critical sources in the patient's current mental status and life history.

d. *Identifying currently active triggering events.* Next comes the search for the most compelling triggers to which the patient is adapting. As noted, they typically have two essential attributes: first, they are, as a rule, frame-related interventions by the therapist; and second, they have, therefore, elicited predatory (in the case of frame modifications) or existential (in the case of frame-securing efforts) forms of death anxiety.

Patients almost always repress critical triggers and/or the most disturbing meanings of triggers, so the trigger search is a critical part of the exercise. As described in Chapter 7, this pursuit is carried out in two ways: first, through efforts at direct recall, or trying to remember what the therapist has done of late in connection with the ground rules of the therapy; and second, by using the themes in the narrative pool as clues to missing triggers. The goal is to identify the most powerfully active, frame-related triggering events and to formulate their implications as a preparation for linking to the bridging and power themes in the patient's narrative pool.

e. *The linking process.* The final step in the self-processing exercise involves linking the themes to their triggers as reflections of the patient's person-

Dream Psychotherapy

ally selected, valid unconscious perceptions of the triggering events. The main obstacles to this effort are:

   i.   A failure to identify the most critical triggering event with which the patient is coping. If this is the case, the themes will not decode easily around the trigger selected by the patient (or later in the session, by the therapist). When this happens, the patient (or therapist) should seek another, more cogent trigger that better fits the themes.

   ii.   A failure to generate good bridging and/or ample power themes. In this case, the patient must go back to the dream for fresh narrative-guided associations; almost always, this second effort is highly productive.

        The linking process generates deep unconscious insight that is then used to clarify the basis for active patient indicators. When necessary, the encoded themes also should be used as directives to rectify a modified frame, that is, to correct an errant ground rule at the behest of the patient's encoded directives.

10. As indicated, once the 40 minutes allotted to the patient have expired, the therapist works with the patient to help him or her to modify the inevitable resistances that have emerged in the course of trying to carry out this process to a suitable end point. If the patient fails to arrive at an available trigger-decoded insight, the therapist should offer the interpretations and frame rectifications called for by the patient's material. The images and themes that follow these interventions are then explored for their validating and meaning fea-

tures. Interventional efforts by both patients and therapists must obtain encoded validation in order to be considered correct and deeply helpful. The absence of deep unconscious confirmation should inspire a search for sources of error. Most often, the error arises from having used the wrong trigger for the linking process.

The essence of this process is, then, the report of a dream; the development of narrative-guided associations; the recognition of patient indicators; the identification of the most active triggering events; the linking of themes to triggers to generate deep insight, and, if need be, to secure deviant aspects of the ground rules; and, finally, the search for encoded validation.

Clinical Illustration

The following is an excerpt from a dream psychotherapy, self-processing session.

Janet Jensen was a 32-year-old married woman in dream psychotherapy with Simon Teller, a therapist. Her primary problems lay in her relationship with her husband, with whom she was very distant and was often afraid of for no evident reason. Of note in her history were two early-stage miscarriages in the initial years of her marriage; she was childless.

Near the end of the first session in this sequence, there was a knock on the door to the consultation room. Dr. Teller arose from his chair and went to the door, where the patient could hear him speaking to another man. The therapist then closed the door and returned to his chair with a package in his hand, which he set on the floor next to him. The session, which Dr.

Dream Psychotherapy

Teller extended for the minute that had been lost, was over before the patient could make any substantial direct or indirect comment on the intrusion.

Mrs. Jensen began the next session with the following dream.

> She is with her girlfriend, Judy. They are eating lunch. A tall, lean man comes to their table and starts to yell at Judy. He's angry at her because she stood him up on a date. He grabs Judy by the arms and shakes her. There was more to the dream, but Mrs. Jensen was unable to recall what it was.

The main guided associations to the dream began with Judy. Mrs. Jensen recalled having had lunch with her on the day after Judy had been assaulted and nearly raped in her apartment by a man who entered through an open window. Judy blamed herself for her carelessness and stupidity in leaving the window unlocked, vowing that she'd never do anything like that again. Mrs. Jensen had tried to reassure her friend, but actually agreed with her—leaving the window unlocked was an invitation to disaster.

Mrs. Jensen said that the incident with Judy brought to mind a horrible story she had read in the newspaper on the day of the dream. It was about a family that was vacationing in the mountains. They had left the back door to their cabin unlocked and the six-year-old daughter had been abducted and killed by a man whom the police later found wandering in the area. "No one's safe anywhere," Mrs. Jensen commented.

> [Omitted here are the other narrative tales that came to Mrs. Jensen's mind as she moved from one element of the dream to another.]

187

DREAMS AND EMOTIONAL ADAPTATION

After telling these stories, the patient went to her self-indicators, noting that she had been unusually mistrustful of her husband that week. She felt hemmed in by him and one night had slept in another room. She said she had no idea what was bothering her about him. As for the therapy, she could think of no way in which she had had an impact on its frame—she had neither modified nor secured any of the ground rules.

Mrs. Jensen made an effort to identify the triggers that were currently active in her therapy, but had considerable difficulty with this part of the exercise. She recalled a background trigger that involved Dr. Teller's accidentally extending a session by five minutes about two months earlier. Other than that, she was sure he'd kept to all of the ground rules and that her sessions were secure from frame deviations.

The patient's assessment of her triggers led her to wonder whether her dreams and associations might not be a reflection of some kind of secured-frame death anxiety, a fear of being trapped by someone and murdered. She admitted that this self-interpretation sounded intellectualized and saw that there were no images that affirmed a secured therapy space.

When the patient's 40 minutes of self-processing were over, Dr. Teller asked her to assess her exercise.

[This is the standard initial comment when the therapist begins to speak. In doing the overview, the patient is asked to determine whether or not he or she had arrived at a punch line—a trigger-decoded insight. If not, the effort is made to identify what led to the failure to complete the process, so as to enable the patient to go back to the exercise to fill in the missing pieces and steps.]

Mrs. Jensen responded that she realized that she hadn't reached a satisfactory punch line, that she hadn't done any

188

Dream Psychotherapy

linking. She seemed to be missing a clear trigger for her power themes; she needed a stimulus for her strong unconscious perceptions. She reviewed the images and identified themes of intruders, violence, rape, harm, murder, and death. With Dr. Teller's help, the patient also recognized themes of unlocked windows and doors, and she noticed now that the murderer was a man and the victim a little girl. In all, the patient saw that her images alluded to violated frames and spoke for some kind of frame violation within the therapy, but she still had no idea what the trigger was.

With help through further questions from Dr. Teller, the patient eventually went back to her dream for some fresh guided associations.

[This is a way of enlisting the help of the deep unconscious system by generating new thematic clues to facilitate the search for a missing trigger.]

The main additional story was connected with the man in the dream who was angry about having been being stood up. Mrs. Jensen recalled an incident from her childhood in which her family physician's office was invaded by a disgruntled former patient who felt that the doctor had harmed him in the course of repairing a hernia. The man had broken into the office and held the doctor and one of his patients hostage. The police arrived and matters got very tense, but eventually they convinced the man to surrender.

Mrs. Jensen reviewed these new themes and tried to use them to discover her missing trigger, but all she could come up with was an occasion, about a year earlier, when she was in a restaurant and Dr. Teller entered with a woman the patient assumed to be his wife. This old trigger certainly could not account for the appearance of these themes in the current session. And Mrs. Jensen knew that her power themes and images of frame violations were addressing an active trigger—they were a reliable indicator of a missing trigger and needed to be accounted for.

Dr. Teller played back a selection of the themes to which the patient had alluded, stressing the images of male invaders and the intrusion into a doctor's office. With a start, Mrs. Jensen suddenly remembered the incident of the previous week in which a man had entered the waiting room, knocked on the door to the consultation room, and given Dr. Teller a package. Amazed that she had forgotten the incident, she could see that this trigger was strongly connected to the themes in her narrative pool (her encoded theme complex): she must have experienced the man as a dangerous intruder and felt violated.

With time running out, Dr. Teller also connected some of the other power themes to the incident: Mrs. Jensen had felt endangered and that her life was threatened. The patient then connected the death of the child to her belief that one of her miscarriages had been caused by her husband's having engaged her in forceful intercourse on the day before she lost the fetus. Dr. Teller added that the invasion by the man must have been experienced unconsciously by her as a similar sexually intrusive attempt at murder. He also noted that the patient had offered a correction—a model of rectification—to the effect that, as was said about Judy's window, the door should be locked to protect her from such invasions and harm, a suggestion that he would take under advisement.

Later that day, Dr. Teller changed the lock on his door so that he could secure it in a way that would keep outsiders from entering his office, and yet would allow his patients to turn the handle from within and readily leave after their sessions had ended. When he went into the waiting room to greet

Dream Psychotherapy

Mrs. Jensen for her next session, he locked the door before following her into the consultation room. The patient turned around and noticed what Dr. Teller had done. Once in the consultation room, she began her session with the following dream.

> She is in a school gymnasium and is teaching children gym exercises when the fire alarm rings and they all file out of the school.

The patient's main guided associations to this dream centered around two stories. The first had to do with a gym teacher in college who had befriended the patient at a time when she was thinking of dropping out of school. The teacher had counseled her and helped her to get over a crisis with a boyfriend that caused her to become depressed and want to flee. Mrs. Jensen still corresponded with the teacher and saw her from time to time; she said she was the best and most helpful teacher she had ever had.

The second story concerned an incident she had seen on television that week, in which a deranged man had burst into a gymnasium and had held a dozen children hostage. He then randomly fired into the group and killed one of the children before turning the gun on himself and committing suicide.

With much help from Dr. Teller, and with considerable anxiety and difficulty on Mrs. Jensen's part, these death-related power themes eventually were linked to the frame-securing trigger constituted by Dr. Teller's acknowledgment of the need to lock his office door, and his subsequent locking of the outer door to his office (the guided associations to the dream came after this intervention). The patient had experienced these frame-securing interventions as exceedingly constructive and helpful—unconscious perceptions that were encoded in the story of the gym teacher.

But the frame-securing triggers also were experienced as entrapping and potentially annihilating, a deep unconscious impression that was based on the miscarriages Mrs. Jensen had had; they were seen as the murder of the entrapped fetuses, and she held not only her husband responsible for what had happened, but herself as well. She had been depressed and suicidal at the time and had ruminated a lot about the senselessness of life.

The breaking and then securing of the frame in this instance had produced both persecutory and existential death anxieties in this patient. Both issues became available for insightful processing.

Summing Up

1. Dream psychotherapy offers patients a maximal opportunity to enter and understand their world of deep unconscious experience.
   a. This includes a sound appreciation of the nature and effects of their therapists' interventions and of major life traumas, as well as insight into their own means of adapting to the conflicts and issues they raise.
2. The structure of dream psychotherapy calls for patients' beginning each hour-and-a-half session by reporting a dream or a spontaneously created story.
   a. There follows, in sequence, guided narrative associations to the elements of the dream until a strong pool of themes has been created; the identification of self-indicators, ways in which the patient has impinged on the ground rules of the therapy toward securing or modifying its frame; the rec-

Dream Psychotherapy

ognition of the therapist's currently active frame-related interventions, the triggers that have evoked the narrative themes; and, finally, the linking and decoding of the themes by connecting them with their evocative triggers so as to interpret the patient's deep unconscious experience and adaptive processing efforts.

3. Dream psychotherapy enables both patients and therapists to experience and appreciate the enormous complexities and richness of dream communication and human emotional adaptation.

Concluding Comments

The morbid qualities of Mrs. Jensen's dream therapy sessions are typical of certain crucial sessions that occur in the course of communicative and empowered psychotherapy. Most often they are, as seen here, the result of significant frame-modifying and frame-securing interventions by the therapist. The latter type of experience is especially crucial to enabling patients to cope with the basic anxieties connected with both life and death. The secured frame's positive sense of holding combines with a dread of annihilation that expresses the essence of life, which is a marvelous gift that inevitably must end in personal tragedy. Indeed, secured-frame anxieties are among the most dreaded affects experienced by humans.

The opportunity to work through and adapt better to these universal and personal issues is unique to communicative and dream psychotherapies, and one of their most salutary features. Such working through is not possible without power themes and extensive explorations of the triggers that are bringing these issues to life in patients in ways that render their responsive adaptations open to constructive transformation and resolution. This kind of effect does not occur with intellectualized discussions of these problems, nor is it possible without trigger-decoding efforts.

To sum up the themes of this book, we can see that dreams are so rich in structure and function that they illuminate every known level of emotional life and emotionally charged human experience and communication—from the behavioral to the deep unconscious. Every psychotherapist must choose the levels at which he or she wishes to work, but doing so within a strong adaptive framework seems essential. By keeping conscious and deep unconscious adaptation center stage, a therapist is in a position to offer his or her patients the best possible therapeutic experiences they could hope for or have. No patient can ask for more, and no therapist can do more for his or her clients and patients.

References

Arlow, J., & Brenner, C. (1964). *Psychoanalytic Concepts and the Structural Theory*. New York: International Universities Press.

Badcock, C. (1986). *The Problem of Altruism: Freudian–Darwinian Solutions*. Oxford: Blackwell.

Badcock, C. (1990a). Is the Oedipus complex a Darwinian adaptation? *Journal of the American Academy of Psychoanalysis*, 18:368–377.

Badcock, C. (1990b). *Oedipus in Evolution*. London: Blackwell.

Badcock, C. (1994). *PsychoDarwinism: The New Synthesis of Darwin and Freud*. London: Harper Collins.

Bickerton, D. (1990). *Language and Species*. Chicago: University of Chicago Press.

Bion, W. (1977). *Seven Servants: Four Works by Wilfred R. Bion*. New York: Jason Aronson.

Campbell, D. (1974). Evolutionary epistemology. In *The Philosophy of Karl Popper, Vol I*, P. Schilipp (Ed.), pp. 413–463. LaSalle, Ill.: Open Court.

Clark, W. (1995). *At War Within: The Double-Edged Sword of Immunity*. New York: Oxford University Press.

Corballis, C. (1991). *The Lopsided Ape*. New York: Oxford University Press.

Dawkins, R. (1976). *The Selfish Gene*. New York: Oxford University Press.

Dawkins, R., & Krebs, J. (1978). Animal signals: Information or manipulation? In *Behavioral Ecology*, J. Krebs & N. Davies (Eds.), pp. 282–309. Oxford: Blackwell.

Dennett, D. (1995). *Darwin's Dangerous Idea*. New York: Simon & Schuster.

Donald, M. (1991). *Origins of the Modern Mind*. Cambridge, Mass.: Harvard University Press.

Elgert, K. (1996). *Immunology: Understanding the Immune System*. New York: Wiley-Liss.

References

Freud, S. (1895). Project for a scientific psychology. *Standard Edition*, 1: 283–397.

Freud, S. (1900). The interpretation of dreams. *Standard Edition*, vols. 4 and 5.

Freud, S. (1915/1985). *A Phylogenetic Fantasy: Overview of the Transference Neuroses* (trans. A. Hoffer & P. Hoffer). Cambridge, Mass.: Harvard University Press.

Freud, S. (1923). The ego and the id. *Standard Edition*, vol. 19.

Gazzaniga, M. (1992). *Nature's Mind*. New York: Basic Books.

Gould, S., & Lewontin, R. (1979). The spandrels of San Marco and the panglossian paradigm. A critique of the adaptationist programme. *Proceedings of the Royal Society of London*, 250: 281–282.

Haskell, R. (1989). Analogical transforms: A cognitive theory of the origin and development of equivalence transformations. *Metaphor and Symbolic Activity*, 4:247–277.

Hauser, M. (1996). *The Evolution of Communication*. Cambridge, Mass.: MIT Press.

Hobson, J. (1988). *The Dreaming Brain*. New York: Basic Books.

Jung, C. (1961). *Freud and Psychoanalysis*. Princeton, N.J.: Princeton University Press.

Jung, C. (1974). *Dreams*. Princeton, N.J.: Princeton University Press.

Krebs, J., & Dawkins, R. (1984). Animal signals: Mind reading and manipulation. In *Behavioral Ecology*, J. Krebs & N. Davies (Eds.), pp. 380–402. Sunderland, Mass.: Sinauer.

Kuhn, T. (1962). *The Structure of Scientific Revolution*. Chicago: University of Chicago Press.

Lakoff, G. (1997). How unconscious metaphorical thought shapes dreams. In *Cognitive Science and the Unconscious*, D. Stein (Ed.), pp. 89–120. Washington, D.C.: American Psychiatric Press.

Langs, R. (1982). *Psychotherapy: A Basic Text*. New York: Jason Aronson.

Langs, R. (1986). Clinical issues arising from a new model of the mind. *Contemporary Psychoanalysis*, 22:418–444.

Langs, R. (1987a). A new model of the mind. *Yearbook for Psychoanalysis and Psychotherapy*, 2:3–33.

Langs, R. (1987b). Clarifying a new model of the mind. *Contemporary Psychoanalysis*, 23:162–180.

Langs, R. (1988). *Decoding Your Dreams*. New York: Ballantine Books.

References

Langs, R. (1992a). *A Clinical Workbook for Psychotherapists*. London: Karnac Books.

Langs, R. (1992b). 1923: The advance that retreated from the architecture of the mind. *International Journal of Communicative Psychoanalysis and Psychotherapy*, 7:3–15.

Langs, R. (1992c). *Science, Systems and Psychoanalysis*. London: Karnac Books.

Langs, R. (1993). *Empowered Psychotherapy*. London: Karnac Books.

Langs, R. (1994). *The Dream Workbook*. Brooklyn, N.Y.: Alliance.

Langs, R. (1995a). *Clinical Practice and the Architecture of the Mind*. London: Karnac Books.

Langs, R. (1995b). Psychoanalysis and the science of evolution. *American Journal of Psychotherapy*, 49:47–58.

Langs, R. (1995c). *The Daydream Workbook*. Brooklyn, N.Y.: Alliance.

Langs, R. (1996a). Mental Darwinism and the evolution of the emotion-processing mind. *American Journal of Psychotherapy*, 50:103–124.

Langs, R. (1996b). *The Evolution of the Emotion Processing Mind: With an Introduction to Mental Darwinism*. London: Karnac Books.

Langs, R. (1997). *Death Anxiety and Clinical Practice*. London: Karnac Books.

Langs, R. (Ed.) (1998a). *Current Theories of Psychoanalysis*. Madison, Conn.: International Universities Press.

Langs, R. (1998b). *Rules, Frames and Boundaries in Psychotherapy and Counselling*. London: Karnac Books.

LeDoux, J. (1996). *The Emotional Brain*. New York: Simon & Schuster.

Lewontin, R. (1979). Sociobiology as an adaptationist program. *Behavioral Science*, 24:5–14.

Lieberman, P. (1991). *Uniquely Human*. Cambridge, Mass: Harvard University Press.

Little, M. (1951). Counter-transference and the patient's response to it. *International Journal of Psycho-Analysis*, 32:32–40.

Lloyd, A. (1990). Implications of an evolutionary metapsychology for clinical psychoanalysis. *Journal of the American Academy of Psychoanalysis*, 18:286–306.

Maidenbaum, A. (1998). Dreams and other aspects of Jungian psychology. In *Current Theories of Psychoanalysis*, R. Langs (Ed.). Madison, Conn.: International Universities Press.

References

Mayr, E. (1983). How to carry out an adaptationist program. *American Naturalist*, 121:324–334.

Mithen, S. (1996). *The Prehistory of the Mind*. London: Thames & Hudson.

Nesse, R. (1990a). Evolutionary explanations of emotions. *Human Nature*, 1:261–289.

Nesse, R. (1990b). The evolutionary functions of repression and the ego defenses. *Journal of the American Academy of Psychoanalysis*, 18:260–285.

Nesse, R., & Lloyd, A. (1992). The evolution of psychodynamic mechanisms. In *The Adapted Mind*, J. Barkow, L. Cosmides, & J. Tooby (Eds.), pp. 601–624. New York: Oxford University Press.

Ornstein, R. (1991). *The Evolution of Consciousness*. New York: Prentice-Hall.

Pinker, S. (1994). *The Language Instinct*. New York: Morrow.

Pinker, S., & Bloom, P. (1990). Natural language and natural selection. *Behavioral and Brain Sciences*, 13:707–784.

Plotkin, H. (1994). *Darwin Machines and the Nature of Knowledge*. Cambridge, Mass.: Harvard University Press.

Plotkin, H. (1997). *Evolution in Mind*. London: Penguin Press.

Raney, J. (1984). Narcissistic defenses and the communicative approach. In *Listening and Interpreting*, J. Raney (Ed.), pp.465–490. New York: Jason Aronson.

Rose, S. (1998). *Lifelines: Biology Beyond Determinism*. New York: Oxford University Press.

Slavin, M., & Kriegman, D. (1992). *The Adaptive Design of the Human Psyche*. New York: Guilford.

Smith, D. (1991). *Hidden Conversations: An Introduction to Communicative Psychoanalysis*. London/New York: Tavistock/Routledge.

Smith, D. (1998). The communicative approach. In *Current Theories of Psychoanalysis*, R. Langs (Ed.). Madison, Conn.: International Universities Press.

Stein, D. (Ed.) (1997). *Cognitive Science and the Unconscious*. Washington, D.C.: American Psychiatric Press.

Szasz, T. (1962). The problem of privacy in training analysis. *Psychiatry*, 25:195–207.

Tooby, J., & Cosmides, L. (1990). On the universality of human nature

References

and the uniqueness of the individual: The role of genetics and adaptation. *Journal of Personality*, 58:17–67.

Winston, A., & Winston, B. (1998). Core conflict theory. In *Current Theories of Psychoanalysis*, R. Langs (Ed.). Madison, Conn.: International Universities Press.

Name Index

Arlow, J., 40, 195

Badcock, C., 12, 13, 85, 195
Bickerton, D., 89, 195
Bion, W., 60, 195
Bloom, P., 89, 198
Brenner, C., 40, 195

Campbell, D., 85, 195
Clark, W., 118, 195
Corballis, C., 89, 195
Cosmides, L., 8, 13, 83, 86, 198

Dawkins, R., 8, 82, 84, 89, 94, 195, 196
Dennett, D., 8, 82, 84, 195
Donald, M., 48, 52, 86, 89, 92, 195

Freud, S., vii, xii, 10, 19, 33, 35, 38, 40, 47, 116, 196

Gazzaniga, M., 48, 86, 196
Gould, S., 8, 9, 83, 196

Haskell, R., 27, 81, 196
Hauser, M., 89, 92, 94, 96, 196
Hobson, J., 5, 24, 196

Jung, C., 33, 196

Krebs, J., 89, 94, 195, 196
Kriegman, D., 7, 9, 12, 41, 84, 85, 86, 198
Kuhn, T., 31, 196

Lakoff, G., 27, 196
Langs, R., viii, ix, 3, 4, 6, 7, 9, 10, 11, 12, 13, 15, 30, 31, 33, 38, 39, 40, 41, 42, 47, 48, 49, 50, 52, 53, 57, 72, 86, 89, 94, 101, 118, 120, 125, 175, 179, 180, 196, 197
LeDoux, J., 49, 90, 197, 198
Lewontin, R., 8, 9, 83, 86, 196, 197
Lieberman, P., 89, 92, 96, 197
Little, M., 38, 197
Lloyd, A., 12, 13, 197, 198

Maidenbaum, A., 23, 197
Mayr, E., 8, 9, 82, 83, 198
Mithen, S., 48, 52, 86, 87, 198

Nesse, R., 12, 13, 94, 198

Ornstein, R., 89, 198

Pinker, S., 89, 198
Plotkin, H., 8, 82, 84, 85, 88, 93, 101, 198

Raney, J., 31, 48, 198
Rose, S., 8, 85, 198

Name Index

Slavin, M., 7, 9, 12, 41, 84, 85, 86, 198
Smith, D., viii, 11, 47, 198
Stein, D., 26, 48, 198
Szasz, T., 38, 198

Tooby, J., 8, 13, 83, 86, 198

Winston, A., 41, 199
Winston, B., 41, 199

Subject Index

Adaptation, 8–17
  conscious, xi
  Freud's problems with, 10–12
  positions on:
    strong, 11–15, 16, 47–62, 79
    weak, 9–11, 16, 37, 79
  unconscious (deep unconscious), xi
  See also Dreams, and adaptation
Adaptationist programs, for
    dreams: *See* Evolution, theory
    of
Affects: *See* Emotions

Biology, 5–9, 11–12, 15
  and psychoanalysis (and
    psychotherapy), 7, 15

Communicative approach, viii–ix,
  16, 31, 50–54, 55–58, 65

Death, 138, 191
  anxiety, 180
    existential, 118, 124–125, 180
    predatory, 88, 118–119, 180
  -related traumas, 56, 124
Deception, as an adaptive strategy,
  88–89, 94–95
Decoding, trigger-based: *See*
  Trigger decoding
Denial: *See* Emotion-processing
  mind, denial by

Dreams
  adaptive approaches to, 54–55,
    63–81
  and adaptation, viii, xiii, 3, 13–
    17, 86–89
    See also Adaptation
  and biology, 7–9
  and ground rules: *See* Ground
    rules, of psychotherapy
  and theories (models) of the
    mind,
    nondynamic, 18–29
    psychodynamic, 30–46
      See also Mind, emotional,
      models of
  and unconscious wishes and
    fantasies, 36–37
  as a form of psychotherapy: *See*
    Psychotherapy, dream
    (empowered)
  as messengers, 3, 66
  as narratives or stories: *See*
    Narratives
  day's residues for, 10, 116
    See also Triggers
  decoding of: *See* Trigger
    decoding, of dreams
  definitions of, 4–7, 13–17, 66
    adaptation-oriented, 12–13, 15,
      16–17, 66
    comprehensive, 13–15
    distal, 14–15

203

Subject Index

Dreams (*continued*)
neuroscientific, 5
phenomenological, 4
proximal, 14
evolution of, 4–5, 82–102, 108–111
adaptationist program for, 83–102
See also Evolution, theory of
examples of (fictional), 22, 67, 102, 126, 138, 144, 164, 187
Freudian theory of, xii–xiii, 10–11, 31–43
structural, 40–43
topographic, 33–40
guided associations to, 98, 130, 164–165, 183, 189, 191
in psychotherapy, xi–xii
Jungian theory of, 23, 31, 32, 43–44
latent contents of, x, 34–35, 42
encoded, x, 54, 66, 76, 100, 120, 125
implications, 54
manifest meanings (contents) of, x, xiii, 54, 66, 68, 71, 76, 120, 125, 135–156
and conscious system, 135
and known triggers, 143, 145–148
and life situations, 143, 150
and patient's emotional self, 148–150
and the status of a psychotherapy, 143, 150–153
therapeutic value of, 143–156
meaning in, 67–71
mechanisms that create, 35
condensation, 35, 97–99
displacement, 35

repression, 35
symbolization, 35
structure of, 76–77
themes in, 59, 74–76, 169–170
bridging (to triggers), 74, 130
See also Themes
trigger decoding of: *See* Trigger decoding, of dreams
Dreamwork, vii, 16, 42, 115–194

Emotion-processing mind, viii, 14–15, 50–54, 78–79, 90–92, 93–96
as Mental module: *See* Modules, mental
conscious system of, 50–51, 52–53, 94
deep unconscious system of, 51–52, 56, 94, 160–162
experiences of, 157, 160–162
denial by, 15, 52
design of, 16, 47–49, 50–54
defensive aspects, 14–15, 52, 55, 93–96, 100–101, 167, 181, 183
repression by, 15, 52
superficial unconscious system of, 51, 56
Emotions, 49, 90
Environment, 6
Events in, as impingements or emotionally charged triggers, ix, 48, 55, 57–58, 167
See also Triggers
Evolution, theory of, 7–9, 15, 84–86
adaptationist program for dreams, 86–102
and dreams: *See* Dreams, evolution of

204

Subject Index

distal dimension (historical), 8–9, 14–15, 17, 84–102
proximal dimension (adaptation), 9, 14, 15, 17
See also Adaptation
psychoanalytic (evolutionary psychoanalysis), 12–13
See also Language

Ground rules, of psychotherapy, 71–76, 78–79, 103–108, 121–126, 140–142
confidentiality, 71–76, 141, 153–155
fees, 126–132, 141–142, 162–163, 165–167
length of sessions, 163–167
modified, 124–125, 168, 186
nature of (ideal), 122–123
nonneutral interventions, 103–108
privacy, 71–76, 141, 153–155, 186–192
relative anonymity, 103–108
secured, 122–123, 153–155, 168
securing (rectifying), 159, 190–192
See also Trigger decoding, and securing the frame (ground rules)

Immune system, 118
Interpretations: See Trigger decoding, and interpreting
Interventions
levels of, 20–22
behavioral, 21, 24–26
brain, 21
cognitive, 21, 26–28
deep unconscious, 21
superficial unconscious, 21

Language
and emotion-related communication, vii, 124
evolution of, 85, 89, 92, 96, 124–125
Linking process, the (linking triggers to themes), 171–177, 184–185

Mind
emotional, models of, 19–20
as brain, 5, 24
as user of universal symbols, 23–24
behavioral, 24–26, 77–78
cognitive, 26–28, 78
communicative: See Emotion-processing mind
Freudian, 78
structural, 40–43
topographic, 33–40, 47
interpersonal, 41, 78
Jungian, 43–44
unconscious, 33–39, 47
emotion-processing: See Emotion-processing mind
Modules, mental, ix, 47–49, 86–89

Narratives
as encoded messages, 64–67
dreams as, vii, xiii, 59, 64–67, 96, 98–99
evolution of, 91–92, 96

Perception, unconscious, xi, 52, 55, 73–76
Psychotherapy, dream (empowered), 179–194
structure of (format), 181–186

205

Subject Index

Repression: *See* Emotion-
processing mind, repression by

Stimuli, emotionally charged: *See*
Triggers

Themes, 169–170
bridging, 169–170
power, 170, 189, 190
in dreams: *See* Dreams, themes
in
Transference, 10, 12, 36
Trigger decoding:
and interpreting, 158, 171–177
examples of, 159, 172, 173,
174
and securing the frame (ground
rules), 159, 173, 176
See also Ground rules, of
psychotherapy
of dreams, xiii, 50, 57–58, 60,
99, 106–108, 127–132
steps in carrying out, 158
Triggers, xiii, 57, 66, 69–76, 103–
108, 115–134, 158, 161, 162–
166, 167–169, 184
classifications of, 119–125

communication of, 168–169
definition of, 116–119
for conscious system (manifest
contents), 118–119, 120, 121–
126, 135
for deep unconscious system
(encoded contents), 120, 121
ground rule interventions as, 71–
76, 103–108, 117–118, 121–
126, 140–142, 153–155
See also Ground rules, of
psychotherapy
known, 139
repressed, search for, 71–73,
1140–142, 153–155, 188–
192
See also: Day's residues;
Environment, events in;
Ground rules, of
psychotherapy

Unconscious perception: *See*
Perception, unconscious

Validation, unconscious, 53, 176
cognitive, 54
interpersonal, 53